T0142571

# A Month of Sundays

*Striding toward Spiritual Refreshment*
*One Sunday at a Time*

Paula Hartman

WESTBOW
PRESS®
A DIVISION OF THOMAS NELSON
& ZONDERVAN

Copyright © 2016 Paula Hartman.
Author of *Real Life Stories* and *Dear Humankind*.

Cover art by Paula Hartman
Cover design by Tyler Cairnes

All rights reserved. No part of this book may be used or reproduced by any means, graphic, electronic, or mechanical, including photocopying, recording, taping or by any information storage retrieval system without the written permission of the author except in the case of brief quotations embodied in critical articles and reviews.

WestBow Press books may be ordered through booksellers or by contacting:

WestBow Press
A Division of Thomas Nelson & Zondervan
1663 Liberty Drive
Bloomington, IN 47403
www.westbowpress.com
1 (866) 928-1240

Because of the dynamic nature of the Internet, any web addresses or links contained in this book may have changed since publication and may no longer be valid. The views expressed in this work are solely those of the author and do not necessarily reflect the views of the publisher, and the publisher hereby disclaims any responsibility for them.

Any people depicted in stock imagery provided by Thinkstock are models, and such images are being used for illustrative purposes only.
Certain stock imagery © Thinkstock.

ISBN: 978-1-5127-3068-5 (sc)
ISBN: 978-1-5127-3069-2 (hc)
ISBN: 978-1-5127-3067-8 (e)

Library of Congress Control Number: 2016903180

Print information available on the last page.

WestBow Press rev. date: 3/15/2016

# CONTENTS

# INTRODUCTION

# Defining Sabbath

I believe it is important to observe Sabbath regularly, not simply because our Creator commanded it but also because it is good for our physical health, our emotional health, and most importantly, our spiritual health. My family consisted of my dad, my mom, my younger sister, my two younger brothers, and me. Because my father was a Methodist minister, observing Sabbath primarily meant going to church on Sunday. This practice was strictly enforced. Once while was I trying to feign illness to get out of going to church, my dad quite simply said, "We are Methodists. On Sunday, Methodists go to church. That is just what we do, so get dressed.

After church my mother usually made a big lunch during which we would critique Dad's sermon. These conversations were rarely about any sort of confusing religious concepts or differing interpretations of biblical scripture. Instead we would meticulously point out every mistake our poor father made during his Sunday morning sermons, especially those made while telling family stories. Dad would try to explain the use of poetic license and the use of embellishment in telling a story. Our mother never allowed us to correct our father in public, but at lunch on Sunday, the game was on.

Until our teenage years, we did not usually watch television on Sunday afternoons. We only had one television. Our dad would sleep the afternoon away in his recliner, the television turned to a political show or another kind of documentary. He would only wake up when we tried to change the channel. So we would just read, play, or do homework until it was time for *Lassie* and the *Ed Sullivan Show*. In later years we replaced early-evening television with attending church youth group. Although Dad taught us a little comparative religion in our confirmation classes and a lot of religious tolerance at home, we observed Sabbath by going to church on Sunday, and I really never really gave it much thought—until I went to college.

I attended a Seventh Day Adventist college my freshman year. I chose it because it had a good reputation for its nursing program as well as its allied health programs. I suddenly found myself living in a dormitory full of Protestants, Catholics, and of course, Seventh Day Adventists, all of us living in close proximity. This was the first time I realized that not everyone's fathers taught them religious tolerance.

For some reason, the Catholic girls and the Seventh Day Adventist girls continually argued about religious concepts and practices in the common kitchen on Friday nights at one or two o'clock in the morning. (Few Protestant girls participated. I guess we, Protestants, just like to sleep.) But it never failed. One of the Catholic girls would wake me up and beg me to help them argue their case against a group of Adventists who could quote Scripture, line and verse. They had apparently confused *preacher's kid* with *biblical scholar*, but I was privy to some lively and emotional debates. One continual subject of discussion was the observance of Sabbath.

My Seventh Day Adventist friends celebrated Sabbath on Saturday, which they considered the seventh day of the week—the day, according to Scripture, that the Creator rested. They believed Sabbath began at sunset on Friday and continued until sundown on Saturday. The observance of their Sabbath included attending church but also prohibited participation in any secular activities, including such things as reading secular books and watching television. This made my non-Adventist friends irate, mostly because few of us had televisions in our rooms. On Friday night, the big television in the common lounge went off at sunset and stayed off until sundown on Saturday.

The angrier my non-Adventist friends became, the more defensive my Adventist friends became. To me, the arguing seemed pointless, so I just learned to roll with it. I went out on Friday nights with my

Catholic and Protestant friends. I went hiking on Saturdays with my new Adventist friends. When I went home for the weekend, I went to church on Sunday. When I stayed at school for the weekend, I went to church on Saturday. I didn't have a car, and the Seventh Day Adventist church was the only one within walking distance.

When I began to compile this book, I decided to do a little research. I thought I should understand more about the origin and evolution of Sabbath before releasing a book about the importance of observing it. I read and read, took copious notes, and read some more. I spent hours following threads of information that clarified nothing. The more I read, the more complicated defining Sabbath became. To be honest, the process was more exhausting than enlightening.

For starters, even the definition of the word *Sabbath* is nuanced. At its simplest, the original Hebrew word for Sabbath means *rest*. To me, this implies rest as in sleeping, lying on the couch, swinging in the hammock, watching television, light reading, and more sleeping. But the Hebrew language is complex, so Sabbath may also be defined as *cessation*. This definition implies a more active type of rest in which regular work and secular pursuits are replaced with activities such as praying, worshipping, spending time outdoors, socializing, sharing meals with family and friends, keeping up marital relations, and sleeping, which still sounds really good to me.

Unfortunately, religious leaders, biblical scholars, theologians, kings, and other governmental makers and shakers have also done a little research on the definition of Sabbath. Actually, they spent centuries developing complicated dogmas and ideologies to define it, and because they apparently had clout and time on their side, they created national laws, religious laws, and social rules to claim authority over its observance. The result was a total lack of consensus. Personally, I just can't believe that our Creator, upon *resting* or *ceasing* from the exhausting work of creating, thought, I'll give them a day off to relax. That will give them something to fight about."

As with my college friends, there was debate surrounding which day of the week we should reserve as the Sabbath, Saturday or Sunday. I was stunned by the amount of material on this subject and also by the intensity with which beliefs about the subject were argued. While many of the discussions were simply explanations of long-held religious traditions, some of the arguments were stated as the irrefutable Word of God. Others implied exclusivity, racism, and anti-Semitism. In my mind, this could almost drive a Creator to drink.

The second major debate was over the definition of work. Does work just mean what you do to make a living? Does work exclude washing the dishes, mowing the grass, or doing laundry? Is making a grocery list or helping a child with a school project considered work? This may sound trite, but there was a time when desecrating the Sabbath was punishable by stoning. I can only imagine someone hauling a wheelbarrow of rocks into his neighbor's yard, saying, "Sorry, buddy, you can't mow the grass today. It's the rule." Traditional Jewish law forbade such things as kindling a fire, so one might think, *Okay, no bonfires on Sabbath*. But it is not that simple. For example, the invention of electricity complicated the law. Is flipping on the kitchen light technically kindling a fire? Does putting your lights on preset timers solve the problem? Like I told you, it's exhausting.

In the primitive Christian church, Christians probably continued to observe Sabbath on Saturday for a period of time. Things changed as the first and second centuries progressed. Over time Sunday became known as the Lord's Day. While Saturday is technically the seventh day of the week, some early Christians began observing Sabbath on Sunday. For the primitive Christian church, the definition of Sabbath began to become a bit confusing.

Ignatius of Antioch, one of the early church fathers, tried to clarify the issue by suggesting that Christians spend Saturday meditating on the law and admiring nature. Ignatius said that preparing food the day before and drinking lukewarm beverages was no longer necessary. So if I understand this church father correctly, cooking was no longer work, and because his letter was written before the advent of the modern refrigeration, a person could apparently kindle a fire if they wanted a hot beverage. He further suggested that Sunday could be revered as the celebration of the resurrection and chief of all days. So, in effect, Sabbath became the entire weekend. I have decided, with all due respect, that Ignatius of Antioch did not have a firm grasp on modern reality and had obviously never been a working mother.

In AD 321, the Roman Emperor Constantine issued a decree making Sunday or what the Emperor called, *The Venerable Day of the Sun*, a day of rest from labor. A provision was made for the cultivation of fields because of heavenly providence. I translated this as the weather.

During my research I found a thread of detail that led to information about the evolution of the modern Western calendar. I will spare you the long story of the transition from the calendar of Romulus, which was created in roughly 753 BC and had 304 days in a year, and the Gregorian calendar, named for Pope Gregory XIII, who introduced it in AD 1585. This calendar has 365.2425 days. The whole leap day ordeal was just too complicated to understand, let alone explain. I feel I should add that our modern Gregorian calendar was not fully adopted by all European countries until AD 1923 and finally by the Soviet Union in AD 1929. If the countries of world were not able to fully agree on how many days there were in a year until 1929, how did we know for sure what day of the week it was? And don't even get me started on the Hebrew calendar.

I understand the complexity of history. I am not poking fun at anyone's religious beliefs or traditions. I understand how important they are, and I know that their observance can bind people together. I am just pointing out how complicated we human being can make things.

Jesus of Nazareth was criticized for healing on the Sabbath. He addressed his critics by saying, "The Sabbath was made for humankind, and not humankind for the Sabbath" (Mark 2:27a). What he did not say is just as important. He did not say Sabbath was created for the Jews, the Catholics, the Methodists, the Baptists, the Seventh-Day Adventists, the Republicans, the Democrats, Americans, or Italians but for all of humankind. I think the command to observe the Sabbath predates the calendar of Romulus, the Gregorian calendar, and all the calendars in between. Call me a rebel, but I believe the Sabbath is simply a gift from our Creator.

The gift of Sabbath gives us permission to stop and take a breath. It is a touchstone to the divine. It reminds us to take a break from our constant striving, judging, anticipating, and worrying. It allows us the time we need to quiet the constant chatter of our minds. It asks us to simply meet life as it comes, to appreciate our imperfect lives, and to feel at peace for one day or for at least for a little while.

Depending on our personal beliefs and traditions, we can observe the Sabbath on Saturday or Sunday, and if we must work at our place of employment on the weekend. Sabbath can still be fully experienced on a Thursday. Sabbath time is not linear. In spite of our rules to make it complicated, Sabbath does not have to play by our rules. I believe Sabbath arrives any time we purposely, without guilt, step out of our regular routines and intentionally create a space for it. We do not need to be well dressed or in a particularly good mood. We do not even need to be on our best behavior. We only need to show up.

Walk with me through a month of Sundays. I believe that when we least expect it, Sabbath will transform the imperfect into the glorious, the common into the extraordinary, and the mundane into the memorable. And we won't have to throw a single rock.

The stories included in this book were written over the span of a decade. Though maybe slightly embellished, they are all true. No names have been changed to protect anyone. They do not follow the linear calendar, and they skip and digress years of time. There is only one rule—just relax and enjoy.

# ABOUT THE RECIPES IN THIS BOOK

I am not a chef. I have never been to culinary school. Except for watching television cooking shows, I have not taken a real cooking class since Home Economics Four in high school. But I love to cook.

In the 1990s, a Swedish psychologist named K. Anders Ericsson was studying expertise, and he found a high correlation between the hours of intentional practice in a given area and the level of expertise in that area. The ten-thousand-hour theory states that to become an expert in a given area, it takes ten thousand hours of focused practice. This got me thinking.

I probably started cooking with my mother as soon as I could reach the kitchen counter. I also took four years of home economics in high school, which involved a fair amount of cooking. But I am not even going to include my earliest years of cooking in my cooking tally.

I became a wife and mother at the age of nineteen. For me, nineteen came thirty-seven years ago. This is when I started cooking in earnest. Let's do the math. Thirty-seven years is equivalent to 13,505 days. By my own estimate (which is an average of the hours I spent cooking really big dinners, including homemade bread, minus dinners out and trips to my mother's house), I have been practicing focused cooking for more than twenty-seven thousand hours. And this doesn't even include Christmas cookies. So I am not a chef. I am an expert.

As all experts, I have studied with devoted teachers—my mother, my grandmother, my home economics teachers, and numerous others. After my mother's death, I was fortunate enough to inherit a box of recipes handwritten on index cards by my Great-Aunt Mayme. I can only assume that some of these recipes include those of my paternal great-grandmothers. This past year I have been cooking them in earnest.

I've discovered that I already cook versions of many of my aunt's recipes. I also found my aunt's handwriting difficult to read. I had to make substitutions for many ingredients that I could simply not decipher. I would find myself thinking, *Aunt Mayme, what is p … t … g? Could you not press harder with your pencil?* It also took numerous phone calls to figure out what some of the ingredients were.

I've had my best friends try to critique the recipes, sometimes under duress. I received some slightly negative reviews. "The olives are a bit too much." "I could eat it." "Loose the salt shaker." "Way too rich." "What's in it?" For purely health reasons, I also had to leave out, "Melt a little bacon fat in a skillet," from many of the recipes. Thus, adaptations were made. Some recipes were rejected outright. But I found some great new recipes, and it was an adventure for all.

The recipes included in this book are my gift to you. They include the best of my aunt's recipes, adaptations of her recipes, and other family recipes. I have also included some of my own recipes and the adaptations of recipes I have collected from friends. They do not require exotic ingredients and can easily be prepared from a well-stocked pantry. I invite you to try them, adapt them, and make them your own.

Sabbath is a great time to do a little cooking. It is a time for comfort food and dessert. It is a time to create from scratch, to simmer and stew, to fill the house with the incense of home. Sabbath invites us to linger at the table and talk awhile. If the Sabbath finds us alone, the spirit of Sabbath will dine with us.

In a world that too often knows starvation, food is a tangible blessing. The ability to cook a meal that can nourish the soul, as well as the body, is a gift. The opportunity to prepare that meal creatively and to share it with others is a privilege. Remember: these recipes are only a gift. They are not a challenge to complicate your personal Sabbath time. There is always room for takeout. Enjoy.

# The Confession of an Overzealous Director

In this household, the hectic of Christmas marched right into the frantic of Epiphany. Truth be known, I was the one who drove the march much like an impassioned general. Now the troops are malnourished—their very survival dependent on a mutilated ham, a shriveled relish tray, and a nutrition-less cornucopia of Christmas candy. This morning, in desperation, my husband fed our cat chicken noodle soup for breakfast. Our living room marks the primary battle zone. Dust, clutter, and a pile of unfolded athletic socks are winning the war. I feel as though I might be running a low-grade fever. And I have no one to blame but myself.

All that my pastor requested was that I put together a simple nativity pageant for Epiphany Sunday. Simple. That is what he said. He is a very considerate person and not one to intentionally overwhelm anyone. I'm sure his idea of simple was--simple, meaning a dozen or so bathrobes, a little tinfoil, some cardboard, and a few strands of tinsel. But to be quite frank, if simplicity was what he wanted, he really should have called someone else—someone with a better grip on the concept, someone with a little less grandiose imagination, someone not so easily driven into a creative frenzy, someone who does not think that the Nobel Prize for science should go to the inventor of the hot-glue gun.

He apparently doesn't know what my husband knows all too well. Behind this façade of calm normalcy lurks the atomic fusion of a Martha Stewart wannabe and the Tasmanian devil. Creative ingenuity is my

1

drug of choice. Keep your cocaine. Keep your heroin. Give me glitter. Give me glue. Give me a pile of garage-sale junk, a laundry basket of discarded bathrobes, and a box of timeworn Christmas decorations, and then stand back.

I will happily trade much needed sleep for the sheer bliss of sculpting aluminum foil. I will endure cold sores that threaten to devour my face and sport enormous dark circles beneath bloodshot eyes for the intoxication of acrylic paint. I will bear the pain of scissor-induced blisters for the pure satisfaction of cutting corrugated cardboard. I will stubbornly tolerate the mental strain of someone saying, "Mom, I do not have one pair of clean socks that, like, match," "Mom, if I eat one more piece of ham, I am going to hurl," and, "Honey, will a cat eat chicken noodle soup?" for the joy of creating twenty-one unique costumes, three kingly treasures, and a backdrop of starlight. On Epiphany Sunday, the magi will enter our sanctuary in style, even if I am in the hospital. This is simply who I am and who I will continue to be.

While I will admit that my desire to sculpt cardboard occasionally throws my life a bit out of balance, I believe the real problem is a result of other flaws in my personality. I have difficulty saying, "No." I do not delegate well, and I don't seem to have a working knowledge of time management. So occasionally a project does tend to take on a life of its own and totally consume my entire life. But I ask you this: Could Mozart ignore his inner yearning to compose? Of course not. How then can I be expected to ignore my hankering to make frankincense out of amber fish aquarium gravel? Did Mozart worry about unloading the dishwasher, folding underwear, or taking down the Christmas tree while writing *Don Giovanni*? I think not.

Why then should I be asked to justify the quarter inch of soap scum in the bathtub while adorning a scarlet crown with a strand of imitation pearls and a large plastic emerald? Was Mozart forced to create by committee? No. Did some well meaning novice place a movement of *Chopsticks* right in the middle of *The Magic Flute*? No. Why then should I delegate the heavenly host and take the risk of watching my angelic heralds approach the manger of the Lord while wearing hunks of poster board on their heads instead of halos made from artificial-berried garland, gold ribbon, and small battery-operated lights? I rest my case.

Luckily for my neglected family, my health is deteriorating, and it's Sunday afternoon. Like a comma penned into a runaway sentence or a rest placed within a score of music, this day prompts me to pause, breathe, and take a nap. For me, a long nap on Sunday afternoon is an absolute necessity. Actually, it's mandatory. After all, it was the great Creator, the one who created Picasso, Michelangelo, and Martha Stewart who said to all humankind, "Six days you shall paint, glue, and glitter. Six days you shall sew and saw. Six days you shall cut colored paper and mold aluminum foil. But on the seventh day, you shall put aside your brush and chisel, your needle and hot-glue gun, and you shall take a long nap. In six days, I made the heavens, the earth, and the sea (pretty much the whole kit and caboodle), but on the seventh day, I simply relaxed. Therefore, I, your Creator, have set Sunday afternoons aside for napping."

Okay, I know those are not the exact words, but the message is implied. Who am I to argue with the brilliance that wove light from darkness and fashioned a human body from mud? Who am I to ignore the advice of the one who thought of giraffes, pinecones, and kiwifruit? Who am I to disobey the one who taught the silver maple to rest in deep winter and wake in the spring?

Gabriel's wings will simply have to wait. So will Mary's gown, and so will the star of Bethlehem, because this old girl is off to bed! When I wake, I'll run to the grocery store. I'll make a hot meal for my family that does not include ham or peppermint candy. I'll relocate to the sofa and fold a laundry basket full of socks. I'll reassure my family that in one week Epiphany will arrive. Mary, Joseph, the babe, the heavenly host, the star of Bethlehem, a band of shepherds, a flock of sheep, a cluster of sparkling stars, and five wise people from the east will make their appearance. Our lives will return to normal, at least for a while.

Having made that promise, I'll watch the violet shadow of dusk transform the leafless silver maple into a silhouette of black brushstrokes against the sky, and I'll probably think, *Maybe Mary's dress should be violet, and maybe I should make a tree to stand beside the manger. I could make it out of cardboard. Maybe I should have one of the children be a little bird. The children could sing, "All Good Beasts". I'd have to make a cow because there's a cow in the song. I could make a cow out of cardboard.*

3

Resting really isn't the best thing I do!

★★★

The work and commitments of life can make us weary and in need of true rest. We usually recognize this kind of fatigue. What we sometimes fail to recognize is the fatigue induced by activities that we usually consider fun or relaxing. Any activity, be it work or play, can drain us physically or mentally if left unchecked or if pursued in an unbalanced manner. Even watching television can keep us from getting the amount of sleep our bodies require to function well.

Sabbath is a time of rest and renewal. It is an important part of our spiritual health and an essential part of our relationship with our Creator. The manner in which we honor Sabbath time will vary from person to person and from Sabbath to Sabbath. Sometimes we need actual sleep. Sometimes we just need to restore order to our households. Sometimes we need to be alone; and sometimes we need to be with other people.

The first step in honoring Sabbath time is to just pause long enough to ask ourselves, *What do I truly need today? What would really refresh me? What activities have been draining me lately? What can wait until Monday?* Sabbath commands you to pause and ask yourself what rest means to you. The ability to recognize what you truly need is the first gift of Sabbath.

## Sunday Dinner Menu

- Hamburger-Cheese Casserole
- Orange Carrots
- Hello Dolly Cake

# Hamburger-Cheese Casserole

## Ingredients

1 pound (450 g) of lean ground beef
1 onion, chopped
1/2 cup (125 mL) of catsup
salt and pepper to taste
dash of Worcestershire sauce
2 cups (450 g) of cooked rice
8 ounces (225 g) of grated American cheese

## Preparation

Place ground beef and onion in a large skillet. Cook on medium heat until ground beef is well done and onion is tender. Pour off excess fat. Add catsup and Worcestershire sauce. Salt and pepper to taste.

Add cooked rice. Stir in grated cheese. Simmer until cheese has melted. Pour in a serving dish and serve hot.

Serves 8. (Approximately 388 calories per serving.)

Adapted from Mayme Pearson's "Hamburger Casserole."

# Orange Carrots

## Ingredients

1 cup (250 ml) of orange juice
1 clove of garlic, minced
2 (14-ounce) (420 g) cans of carrots, drained
salt to taste
1 tablespoon (15 g) of margarine

## Preparation

In a saucepan, mix orange juice and garlic. Mix well. Add carrots. Bring to a boil and then reduce heat and cook on medium until thickened. Salt to taste. Add margarine. Serve hot.

Serves 6. (Approximately 90 calories per serving.)

Adapted from Mayme Pearson's "Orange Carrots."

# Hello Dolly Cake

## Ingredients

8 tablespoons (120 g) of margarine
1 cup (225 g) of graham cracker crumbs
1 cup (225 g) of coconut flakes (optional)
8 ounces (225 g) of semisweet chocolate chips
1 cup (225 g) of chopped nuts
1 (14-ounce) (420 mL) can of sweetened condensed milk

## Preparation

Melt butter in a 9 × 9 × 2–inch pan. Sprinkle into the pan a layer of each: graham cracker crumbs, coconut flakes, chocolate chips, and chopped nuts. Pour condensed milk over nuts. Bake at 350 degrees F (180 degrees C) for 30 minutes. Cool in pan, and then cut into 16 squares.

Serves 16. (Approximately 287 calories per serving.)

Adapted from Mayme Pearson's "Hello Dolly Cake."

# SUNDAY #2

---

# Behind the Scenes

I was kneeling at the back of sanctuary, script in hand, as the narrator read the words of a familiar story, "And in those days a decree went out from Caesar Augustus that all the world should be taxed."

Teare crept in and whispered, "Paula, the star of Bethlehem just threw up all over her costume. Her mother is taking her home." The situation demanded immediate action. We scurried out of the sanctuary, where twenty (twenty-one if you count my friend Sandy who was in charge of the heavenly host) costumed children stood fidgeting in the foyer. While the faithful sang *Oh Little Town of Bethlehem*, recalling a deep and dreamless night of two thousand years ago, I frantically removed seventy-five bobby pins from the hair of the twelve-year-old girl, previously a member of the heavenly host. I replaced her angelic halo with the celestial orb of the star of Bethlehem.

"Jericha, be careful climbing the ladder," I whispered.

"I will," she replied with the seriousness of a fighter pilot. Her previous job had been to lead the procession of the heavenly host, carrying in her arms the Christ child, who was played by eight-month-old, Emily.

"Matt!" I said in hushed desperation to Jericha's fourteen-year-old brother, also a member of the heavenly host, "do you think you can carry the baby to Mary?"

A look of momentary uncertainty was followed by a grin and a nod. "Sure."

Melanie, the baby's real mother, placed the small robed actress into Matt's arms. "Take this rag in case she spits up."

"Does she spit up a lot?" Matt whispered.

Melanie smiled. "Sometimes she does, Matt." There came another grin and another nod.

I am telling my husband about this as we eat lunch. "Jericha had to step in as the star of Bethlehem, and Matt had to lead the heavenly host and carry Emily. It was tense there for a few minutes. Really tense."

My husband smiles the smile I've come to know well after many years of marriage. It's a cross between *you're so cute when you're excited* and *I wasn't paying one bit of attention to what you were saying, and therefore, I have not the faintest idea about what you just said.*

He replies, "Can you hand me the crackers?"

This doesn't bother me. It's simply a part of the ebb and flow of our lives together. I realize he's had only had one real meal in two weeks. I am aware that he watched a quarter of a Monday night football game, wearing the Virgin Mary's headdress, while I flittered around him with scissors, pins, and a hot-glue gun. I know that he spent most of his Saturday evening transporting props and costumes to the church and that later that same night during a romantic moment, I whispered, "Don't let me forget to grab an extension cord in the morning." I hand him the crackers, kiss the top of his head, and leave him to his soup.

Folding a load of towels from the dryer, I think of eleven-year-old Betsy, a beautiful young girl whose face is almost hypnotic. I think of her dressed head to toe in light blue beside a makeshift manger. I think of her laughing as the child in her lap played peekaboo with her headpiece. I think of her pointing her finger at her Joseph and saying, "Don't step on my robe."

Settling beneath our comforter to nap, I ask my husband, "Do you have my pillow?" and he does. He always has my pillow. The exchange is done without any further need of communication. "I'm just going to read for five minutes," I tell him. He knows this really means, *I am going to leave the light on for about twenty minutes or until I fall asleep midsentence.* As he shuts his eyes, he pats my thigh. This means, "Read as long as you want. I love you. Sleep well." He always does this.

Opening the book I have been reading, one about reorganizing your home, I think of the look in Jericha's eyes as she took on the mission of guiding a group of magi to a stable in our sanctuary. I think of the awkward way Matt took little Emily into his arms and then, like a pro, tucked a spit rag into his angelic belt. I think of the mayhem in the dressing room, where we ran out of safety pins, not realizing it would take forty-seven of them to attach Gabriel's floor-length wings. I think of adorable little Andrew, one of our four-year-old sheep, one with an apparent passion for percussion instruments, ringing the little jingle bell around his neck with enough vigor to out ring a steeple bell.

I think of my friends Tammey, Melanie, and Teare working with the intensity of a pit crew at the Grand Prix. I think of Tammey saying, "Andrew, let me hold your bell for you." I think of Melanie sitting in the front pew just in case baby Jesus became unhappy in her role, wanting only her real mommy. I think of Teari comforting a very sick little star of Bethlehem and of Sandy sparking with the heavenly host. I think of my husband wearing Mary's headpiece and smiling across his soup.

I listen to the familiar mystery of my husband's breathing. I kiss his shoulder. This means, *I'm turning off the light off now. Sleep well. Thank you for simply existing.* This is what I do before I go to sleep, before I drift through the veil of dreamtime into a place where the ordinary and the extraordinary dance together like snowflakes, where paradox and epiphany are as natural as sunlight on snow.

★★★

It's important to occasionally step off stage and pay attention to what is occurring behind the scenes. Life is not merely the performance. It's also the endless rehearsals, some of which go well and some of which don't. It's the arrangement and the rearrangement of props. It's the lost and misplaced props. It's the forgotten lines and missed entrances. It's the costumes that don't fit. It's the songs that suddenly veer off key. It's the trust one cast-member places in another. It's the moment of gut-wrenching panic before the curtain rises.

In the hurry of everyday life, we tend to miss life itself. We listen to others without truly hearing what is said. We become so caught up in meeting our own expectations and the expectations of our society that we ignore subtle flashes of beauty and mystery. We become so preoccupied with every minute distraction and meaningless detail that we lose sight of what makes life feel worth living.

Moments of understanding and insight require downtime—time to simply watch life's passing, time to reflect, time to listen deeply, time to cherish the life we live now with all its imperfections, time to feel the beauty of life pulsing around us and within us, time to look up into a night sky for a single shining star that will lead us to something profound and life-altering. Sabbath time is the gateway to epiphany.

*Paula Hartman*

## Sunday Dinner Menu

- Open-Faced Ham and Cheese Sandwiches
- Green Onion Soup
- Butter Pecan Ice Cream with Homemade Butterscotch

---

## Open-Faced Ham and Cheese Sandwiches

---

### Ingredients

6 slices (60 g) of whole wheat bread
12 slices (60 g) of deli ham per person
6 slices (30 g) of Swiss cheese per person
6 teaspoons (10 g) of margarine or butter per person

### Preparation

Butter bread on one side and place on broiler pan. Broil for about two minutes or until the bread is toasted. Flip the bread over. Place two pieces of ham and one slice of cheese on each piece of bread. Broil for another two minutes or until cheese melts.

Serving size: 1 sandwich (Approximately 256 calories per sandwich.)

Adapted from Mayme Pearson's recipe "Easy Open Faced Broiled Ham and Cheese Sandwiches."

# Green Onion Soup

## Ingredients

1 1/2 cup (338 g) of thinly sliced of green onions and tops
3/4 cup (168 g) of finely chopped celery
2 tablespoons (30 g) of butter or margarine
2 tablespoons (30 g) of flour
2 cups (500 mL) of prepared chicken broth
1 cup (250 mL) of 2 percent milk

## Preparation

In a large saucepan, cook onions and celery in butter for 5 minutes. Gradually blend in flour. Add chicken stock and simmer, stirring frequently until slightly thickened. Simmer 10 minutes. Add milk. Heat through, and serve.

Serves 6 (Approximately 80 calories per serving.)

Adapted from Mayme Pearson's "Green Onion Soup.

# Butter Pecan Ice Cream with Homemade Butterscotch

## Ingredients

6 tablespoons (90 g) of margarine, divided
1/2 cup (125 mL) of milk
2 2/3 cups (375 g) of brown sugar
1 tablespoon (15 mL) of lemon juice

## Preparation

Melt 1/4 cup of butter or margarine. Pour into milk.

In a double boiler, cook buttered milk, brown sugar, and lemon juice on low for 1 hour, stirring occasionally. Serve with ice cream.

Serves 8 (Approximately 222 calories per serving without ice cream.)

Adapted from Mayme Pearson's "Butterscotch Sauce for Ice Cream.

# SUNDAY #3

# Resolving to Not Resolve

I have heard that 80 percent of Americans break their New Year's resolutions and that half of these are broken before the end of January. As most Americans, my past resolutions have been doomed to failure. Two years ago I decided not to drink any more soft drinks, thinking I would be healthier by not eating artificial sweeteners. On the seventh day of that glorious year, I opened the refrigerator door and guzzled half of a two-liter bottle of pop.

Last year I joined the *over thirty club*, getting closer to forty than I am comfortable with, and I am also a member of the I *will eat anything that remains still* group. I decided to lose ten pounds. I did it, sort of. If you tally all the weight I lost during the year, I lost five pounds on a sensible low-fat, high-carbohydrate diet (what I call the *French fry-craving diet*). I lost two pounds this summer when it was nearly 100 degrees for a week. The ceiling fans only kept the moisture from condensing on the furniture, and I lived on crushed ice. I lost four pounds during a bout with intestinal flu. Altogether, I lost eleven pounds.

Yeah for me! Unfortunately, we must add the three pounds I regained after my diet. We must add the three pounds I gained during a little spell of depression around my thirty-sixth birthday. We must also add the five pounds I mysteriously put on between Thanksgiving and Christmas. My grand total lost for year? Zip. Therefore, this year I have resolved to not resolve.

I have though made a resolution of sorts, so technically I may have already broken my resolution to not resolve. My *not a New Year's resolution* is to ever so gently with sincere motherly love and patience nudge my ten-year-old son toward a higher level of self-reliance.

Lately I have come to realize that much of his inability to do things, such as scrape his plate into the trash without adhering little pieces of corn to the wall, empty his pockets before putting his jeans in the wash (so I get to scrape bubble gum off the side of the dryer with a table knife), and replace the toilet paper when the roll is empty, is partially my fault. It is so much simpler to do it myself than to explain for the fourth time how to boil a cup of water in the microwave. He plays dumb, and I take over. He plays dumb, and I do it for him. He plays dumb, and I finish it. It's a mother-son waltz, and he's leading.

I was complaining about the bubble gum incident at work when my boss, Karen, an unmarried woman without children (the kind who usually has ample free advice on both marriage and the proper way to raise children), said, "You know, incompetence can be taught." Ding, ding, and ding! Major light bulb.

I explained my new approach to my husband, asking him to be patient while I let our son flounder through tasks without the benefit of help. His mouth said, "I think you are right." His eyes said, "I can't wait to see this."

Our first attempt at this new mother-son waltz was after dinner. I said, "Mark, please wash the broiler pan."

He countered, "In the sink? Why can't you just put in the dishwasher? This thing is disgusting. Where's the soap? Do I have to use hot water? How hot? Is this hot enough? Is this too much soap? How much water do I put in the sink? Is this enough water? Where's the rag? This is never going to come off. Do I have to wash the top and the bottom? Should I add more soap? Can I use the sprayer to rinse? Is this good enough?"

Somewhere between my sternum and my larynx were the words, *let me do it.* But I resisted. After the pan was washed, I mopped the water from the floor, the cabinet, and the window. I knew I should have made him clean up the mess, but I simply did not have the strength to continue.

Round two was T-bone night. I usually cut my children's steak for them as my mother did for us. (My sister, Leanne, swears to this day that she can barely peel an apple because Mom never let her use a knife.) In keeping with my new resolve, I placed the uncut steak on his plate and the steak knife beside it. Dinner began. Mark picked up his knife and began earnestly sawing away at his steak. After about 4.3 seconds of trying, he asked, "Mom, will you just do this?"

I said, "You can handle it." He sawed and sawed. I did nothing to intervene, except to make a mental plan should he sever an artery. An hour and a half later, Mark was through with his steak. He was sweating. His potato, roll and salad were untouched.

It is Sunday night, Boy Scout night, and it was time for round three. He began by saying, "Mom, have you seen my Boy Scout shirt?"

"It should be in your closet," I replied.

"It's not," he said, and then he added, "You know, I think I stuffed it in my drawer."

A few minutes later, he came into the kitchen, carrying his wrinkled, squashed-up shirt, "Mom, this needs to be ironed." Out of the corner of my eye, I saw my husband smile. This only strengthened my resolve.

With a deep breath, I set up the ironing board, plugged in the iron, and sat out a can of spray starch. "Honey, you shoved your shirt into your drawer, so you iron it." Oh, the disbelief, the terror.

"I don't know how to iron. I am going to burn the tar right out of myself!" he whined as I showed him how to lay the shirt out and begin to iron. He, of course, loved the spray starch. He was spraying it on so heavily it looked like the shirt had been smeared with toothpaste. "Great! Now the whole shirt is wet," he said as if it was my fault.

"Don't hold the can so close to the shirt," I said.

It took almost twenty minutes for Mark to finish ironing his shirt. It was a little damp, and the wall above the ironing board was dripping with spray starch. But as he unplugged the iron, he said with great pride, "Just call me Iron Man."

I am not sure how this whole saga will play out. Best-case scenario, a decade or more from now, my darling new daughter-in-law will call just to tell me what a wonderful husband Mark is and to thank me for raising such a thoughtful, self-sufficient son. Worst-case scenario, raising children will leave me a blathering idiot. I won't be able to cut my own food or take care of my own clothing. When my son asks me to wash the broiler pan, I won't remember what a broiler pan looks like. But for now I will just take a long bath.

★★★

In our complex society, where both parents often work full-time, the work of teaching others to be self-sufficient becomes even more difficult. Everything we do is done on the fly. Household chores are crammed somewhere between too many obligations and too little downtime at home. Sadly, this push and pull can create resentment, anger, and frustration. Sabbath is the perfect time to slow down, regroup, rest, and reconnect with the people we care about.

Today, take an honest and unemotional look at the division of labor in your home. Identify tasks that are unpleasant, exhausting, or simply not yours to shoulder alone. Then gently delegate some of these tasks in the week ahead. Like anything else, delegation takes practice, and practice requires a sense of humor. Don't judge the outcome of others' efforts by your own standards. No white-glove testing. No nagging. Be patient. Teach and reteach as necessary.

Try to outsource some of the more mentally draining or fatigue inducing work. For example, pay someone to mow your grass if you detest doing it. Clear your house of useless items and unwanted clutter so there is less to dust, clean, and worry about. Gracefully back out of or just quit some the activities you do not enjoy or those done out of a misplaced sense of obligation. Encourage family members to do the same. Simplify. Simplify. Simplify.

Most importantly, create space for Sabbath time. Lead by example. Make the observance of Sabbath time a rule for your children. Create a period of time each week when everyone is required to be at home, and then just enjoy being home. Mandate that cell phones and electronic devices remain idle. Read, paint, or play the piano. Do things that you enjoy doing. Intentionally foster a period of time that will teach your children to entertain themselves in creative ways. If they are bored, let them be bored. Continue to let them be bored for a period of time consistently week after week. In the long run, it will be well worth the effort.

## Sunday Dinner Menu

- Ground Beef Sandwiches
- Hot Potato Salad with White Potatoes
- Dressing for Hot Potato Salad
- Easy Lemon Cake

---

# Ground Beef Sandwiches

---

## Ingredients

1 pound (450 g) of ground beef
1/4 cup (60 mL) of olive oil or vegetable oil
1/4 cup (60 g) of diced onion
1/4 cup (60 g) of green peppers, finely diced
1 stalk (30 g) of celery, thinly sliced
1 clove (15 g) of garlic, minced
1 (8-ounce) (225 g) can of mushrooms, drained
1/4 pound (112 g) of American cheese
1 small can (135 g) of tomato paste
1 tablespoon (15 g) of brown sugar
1 tablespoon (15 mL) of Worcestershire sauce
1 (5-ounce) (150 mL) can of tomato juice
salt and pepper
hamburger buns

## Preparation

Brown ground beef and set aside. In a small saucepan, sauté onion, green pepper, and celery in oil until tender. Add garlic and sauté a few minutes longer. Add mushrooms, cheese, tomato paste, brown sugar, Worcestershire sauce, and tomato juice. Add salt and pepper to taste. Cook slowly until thick. When ready to serve, place meat on hamburger buns.

Serves 8. (Approximately 340 calories per serving; includes bun.)

Adapted from Mayme Pearson's "Make Ahead Ground Beef Sandwiches."

# Hot Potato Salad with White Potatoes

## Ingredients

2 pounds (900 g) of small white potatoes
1 teaspoon (5 g) of salt
1 small onion
1 tablespoon (15 g) of minced parsley
1 teaspoon (5 g) of celery seed
2 hard-boiled eggs, chopped
2 tablespoons (60 mL) of olive oil

## Preparation

Wash potatoes. Leaving skins on, place the potatoes into a large saucepan and cover with water. Add salt to water. Bring water to a boil. Turn burner down to medium and cook potatoes until tender. Drain.

Allow potatoes to cool enough to handle. Leaving the skins on the potatoes, cut them into cubes and place them in a serving dish. Add raw onions, parsley, and celery seed. Add dressing and toss lightly with a fork until potatoes are coated with dressing. Garnish with crumbled crisp bacon, if desired. Serve hot.

# Dressing for Hot Potato Salad

## Ingredients

1/2 cup (120 g) of minced onion
2 tablespoons (30 mL) of olive oil
1 1/2 teaspoons (7 g) of flour
1 tablespoon (5 g) of sugar
2 teaspoons (10 g) of salt
1/4 teaspoon (1.2 g) of pepper
1/3 cup (75 mL) of vinegar
1/3 cup (75 mL) of water

## Preparation

In a skillet, sauté minced onion in olive oil until tender, not brown.

In a small mixing bowl, mix flour, sugar, salt, and pepper. Add vinegar and water to bowl. Blend. Stir into onions, and simmer until slightly thickened.

Serves 8. (Approximately 290 calories per serving; includes dressing.)

Adapted from Mayme Pearson's "Hot Potato Salad."

*Paula Hartman*

---
# Easy Lemon Cake
---

## Ingredients

1 box (460 g) yellow cake mix
4 eggs
1 (4-ounce) (120 g) package of sugar-free lemon gelatin
3/4 cup (175 mL) of vegetable oil
3/4 cup (175 mL) of water
1 1/2 cups (338 g) of powdered sugar
1 tablespoon (15 g) of grated lemon peel
juice of 2 lemons
extra powdered sugar for dusting top of cake

## Preparation

Combine cake mix, eggs, lemon gelatin, oil, and water. Beat 4 minutes. Pour into 13 × 9–inch greased baking pan. Bake 40 min. at 350 degrees F (180 degrees C).

Cool for about for about 20 minutes.

In a mixing bowl, mix powdered sugar, grated lemon rind, and lemon juice. Prick the cake with a fork, and pour the lemon mixture over the cake. Dust with powdered sugar.

Serve with whipped cream.

Serves 8–10. (Approximately 466 calories per serving; includes 2 tablespoons [30 g] of whipped cream.)

Adapted from Mayme Pearson's "Easy Lemon Cake.

# SUNDAY #4

# Working on Sunday

The winter sky is a ballet of gemstones. Blue topaz, pink quartz, and mother of pearl dance on tiptoe above the distant tree line. I turn off the radio, silencing a media preacher with a strong Southern accent who seems to be gasping for air.

I work as a lab tech in a blood bank at a large city hospital. My coworkers and I find compatible blood for patients in need of blood transfusions. Our work is specific and repetitive. My coworker Filly tells students and new employees that our job is 90 percent monotony and 10 percent sheer panic with very little room for mistakes. That pretty much sums it up. We rotate weekends, and today it is my turn to pull myself from bed at 5:30 and leave my family, still sleeping, on a Sunday morning. Though I am tempted to feel sorry for myself, the blue of the sky is sincerely blue, and I have a lemon poppy seed coffee cake and a thermos of coffee on the seat beside me. Plus I work with Filly today. I choose to feel blessed.

The morning is slow, as Sundays often are. We finish our routine work quickly, and we each eat two pieces of coffee cake at our boss's desk. (Luckily, our boss understands the need for special treats when working on a Sunday.) Filly is Italian with dark hair and eyes. She always wears red lipstick. She makes me promise that when she is ninety-nine and on her deathbed, I will make certain her lipstick is in place. I remind her that I will be ninety-eight and I'll be suffering the degeneration that runs in my family, so I might be blind or only have a little peripheral vision. Her lipstick might be a little smeared, but I tell her I will do my best. Filly is passionate about her work, her life, and her coffee.

Filly is reading a book, a true story about a group of people who climbed the Himalayan Mountains. Each day I listen as she narrates the latest chapter with impassioned detail. It is like reading a summer novel in installments. This morning one of the climbers has frozen to death, and the other climbers are forced to leave his body behind. She is perched on the edge of her chair, her eyes wildly animated. I find myself thinking that if she has one more cup of coffee, she might rise from her chair and act the book out physically. I love this woman, and I love working with her.

Just as Filly's mountain climber, the one left for dead, comes plodding down the mountain like a frozen zombie, the phone rings. A patient is actively bleeding, and she is on her way to surgery. Our coffee cups are quickly abandoned. Our conversation ceases, and we begin a well-rehearsed litany of movement and language that will continue at a furious pace nonstop until the shift's end. The speed at which we must now function requires a great deal of concentration. We become quiet, absorbed in our work—the same work we do day after day, year after year over and over again. I glance across the bench at Filly. She is focused and flushed. And she is fast. This is when I admire her the most. This is when I love my job the most.

As we leave for home, other hands take up the work we leave at shift's end. We missed lunch, so I am hungry. I do not know if our patient will live through the night. I think of her family waiting uncertain hour after uncertain hour. I have been in their place before.

Turning on the radio, a familiar song full of electric guitar chords reminds me of an earlier time when I thought of myself as a little more immortal than I feel today. As the guitar rises, Ronnie Van Zant and I begin to sing, "If I leave here tomorrow … would you still remember me-ee? I must be traveling on now." I take a slow, deep breath, and the breathing feels good. The sky is sparkling like sunlight on water. My husband has baked potatoes in the oven, and I am going home.

★★★

When our work is done mindfully, it can feel as sacred as worship. Through its familiar litany of language and its ritual of daily duties, work can connect our minds with our bodies, absorbing us like a prayer.

Sabbath invites us to focus on what is meaningful in our work, to focus on what challenges us to do our best, to focus on the positive in what we do, and to dwell on those things. This is not a day for gossip and negativity. It is a day to wear a little red lipstick, to embrace what you do with passion, and to treat coworkers and customers with extra tenderness.

Work can threaten the sanctity of Sabbath, separating us from family, rest, and worship, but if we who must go to the workplace on a Sabbath learn to create that sanctity within our own attitudes, we can become the breath of Sabbath, walking and working in the world.

## Sunday Dinner Menu

- Chopped Steak with Parsley Mushroom Sauce
- Parsley Mushroom Sauce for Chopped Steak
- Baked Potatoes with Butter and Sour Cream
- Granny's Frozen Fruit Salads

---

# Chopped Steak with Parsley Mushroom Sauce

---

## Ingredients

1 pound (450 g) of ground sirloin or lean ground beef
2 eggs, lightly beaten
1/2 sweet onion, chopped
1 clove of garlic, minced
1 tablespoon (15 mL) of Worcestershire sauce
2 tablespoons (30 g) of bread crumbs or finely crushed saltine crackers
1/4 cup (56 g) of flour
1/2 teaspoon (2.3 g) of salt
1/4 teaspoon (1.2 g) of pepper

## Preparation

Preheat oven to 350 degrees F (180 degrees C). Place all ingredients in a large mixing bowl, and mix well. With your hand or the handle of a table knife, score the meat into eight fairly equal servings. Form each serving of ground beef into an oval patty.

In a large nonstick skillet on the stove, brown the patties on both sides (3–4 minutes). Place browned patties in a 13 × 9–inch baking dish. Drain fat from the skillet, reserving browned bits of meat. Pour parsley and mushroom sauce (see following) over patties. Cover with aluminum foil. Bake for 30 minutes at 350 degrees F (180 degrees C). Serve hot.

# Parsley Mushroom Sauce for Chopped Steak

## Ingredients

2 tablespoons (30 g) of margarine or butter
1/4 cup (56 g) of chopped onion
1 can (10 3/4 ounces or 322 g) of condensed mushroom soup
1/4 cup (56 mL) of milk
1 tablespoon (15 g) of chopped parsley
1 (4-ounce) (120 g) can of sliced mushrooms (optional)

## Preparation

In pan containing the browned bits of meat, melt margarine. Cook onion in margarine over low heat until the onion is soft. Add mushroom soup, milk, parsley, and mushrooms. Stir until well blended and hot. Pour over cooked patties, and follow baking instructions in the recipe for chopped steak (see previous).

Serves 8. (Approximately 295 calories per serving; includes chopped steak and sauce.)

Adapted from Mayme Pearson's "Chopped Steak with Parsley-Mushroom Sauce."

# Granny's Frozen Fruit Salads

## Ingredients

2 cups (454 g) of sour cream
2 tablespoons (30 mL) of lemon juice
1/2 cup (120 g) of sugar
1/8 teaspoon (0.5 g) of salt
1 8-ounce (225 g) can of crushed pineapple, well drained.
1 banana, diced
4 drops of red food color
1-pound can (450 g) of Bing cherries, well drained
1/4 cup (56g) of chopped pecans or walnuts
Chocolate ice cream syrup (optional)

## Preparation

In a large bowl, mix sour cream, lemon juice, sugar, and salt until well blended. Add pineapple, banana, food coloring, and cherries, and mix well. Blend in pecans or walnuts. Place in a 9 × 12–inch baking pan or serving dish. Place in freezer until firm (several hours).

When ready to serve, cut into squares. Garnish with a drizzle of chocolate ice cream syrup, if desired.

Serves 10. (Approximately 345 calories per serving.)

Adapted from Ida Bruner's recipe "Frozen Fruit Salad.

# The Origin of Tall Tales

My husband is leaving for a weeklong conference in North Carolina. His work does not require a great deal of travel, but I usually fly solo for a couple of weeks each year. His kiss good-bye includes the promise to call each night, and we go through our usual exchange of warnings and reminders.

- Drive carefully.
- Make sure you lock the doors at night.
- Stop and rest if you get sleepy.
- Take the garbage out Tuesday morning.
- Call me as soon as you get to the hotel.
- Call Tim if you need anything.

Our neighbor, Tim, is a larger-than-life kind of man with a Southern accent as thick as the moustache on his upper lip. He speaks in a voice that reverberates like a base drum. Tim is a hybrid, a cast notable characters—Scout's daddy, Atticus, from *To Kill a Mockingbird*, Jed Clampett of Beverly Hills fame, and the fierce mountain man who scared me to death in the movie *Deliverance*.

In spite of his complex personality and his total inability to whisper, we adore our hillbilly neighbor. And we adore his hillbilly wife, Noreen, who has the voice and hair of a country-western singer and who, even after childbirth, has a figure that could make Miss West Virginia green with envy.

After dinner the kids and I sprawl out on the sofas with blankets and popcorn. We are watching a remake of an Alfred Hitchcock movie. "A classic," I tell them. As a young woman checks into a creepy motel, the phone rings. "Hey, it's Tim. Just called to let you know we'll be home tonight in case you need anything."

"Thanks," I say. "We're fine." The young woman is now screaming in a bloody shower, blocking the knife of an unseen psychotic. I hang up the phone, thinking, *What could happen?*

When my husband went to Chicago a few years back, the pump in our well stopped working. I called the house next door. "Tim, we have no water," I said. In a matter of minutes, he was in our utility room, digging through a gray box of wires with my husband's metal screwdriver. "Tim," I said, "maybe you should shut the power off before you dig around in there." (I must note that Tim has a history of minor electrocutions.)

"Nah," he said as he continued to move the screwdriver through the metal box.

"You know, Tim, I'd really feel better if you'd shut the power off."

He replied sternly, "I know what I'm do ... ZZZZTTTT!" He jerked a bit and mentioned something about the Lord God Almighty.

"Tim!" I said, "are you okay?"

"I'm just fi ... ZZZTTT." He jerked again, this time declaring himself to the son of a floozy.

"Tim!" I pleaded, "please turn the power off before you kill yourself!"

"Why don't you just go upstairs," he ordered, returning to what was quickly becoming a suicide mission.

"Somebody needs to be here to call 9-1-1," I countered.

He imitated me in falsetto voice, "Somebody needs to ... ZZZTTT!" He jerked again, this time mentioning the Lord God Almighty, his mother, the floozy, and a trip to a bathroom in one great booming breath. (I think I recall smiling at this point, but I don't think I was actually laughing.)

"Do you find this funny?" he demanded. He was still twitching.

"I'm sorry," I said, "but if you start digging in those wires again, I'm calling Noreen."

"And just what is Noreen going to do?" he yelled.

"Help me perform CPR!!" I yelled back." It was a standoff.

"Look," he said through clenched teeth, (I wasn't sure if his teeth were clenched because he was mad or because he'd just undergone self-imposed electroshock therapy.) "I'm going to shut the power off now. Go away."

When Tim tells this story, he only gives reference to one mild surge of electricity. He insinuates that I was laughing hard, and he points out the fact that we did have water when he was finished. When I tell the story, there are three distinct jolts of teeth-chattering current and the odor of burning hair. Plus I do great sound effects.

When my husband went to Minneapolis, I woke to find a large furry animal lying facedown in the foyer, a gift from our dog. She had apparently pulled it through the pet door. I could not tell if it was breathing, and I'll admit I made no attempt to go anywhere near it. Instead I grabbed the cordless phone and climbed on top of the kitchen counter. From this position I could keep an eye on the foyer and still feel safe should the animal suddenly leap up the stairs with its teeth exposed.

"Tim, come quick. There's a huge animal in our foyer. I'm not sure if—" Click. The door burst open, and Tim charged into the house. He was carrying his shotgun. "Where is it?" he gasped, almost stepping on it.

"There!" I pointed. He jumped back and then cautiously approached the animal, poking it with the end of his shotgun. It didn't move. He poked it again.

"Why didn't you tell me the thing was dead?" he bellowed.

"I wasn't sure it was dead," I said

"You didn't check?"

"No."

"Why?"

"Because."

He leaned against the door. "I ran over here so fast my knees are weak, and it's dead."

"What if it hadn't been dead?" I ask. "What were you going to do? Shoot it? In the foyer?"

As he turned to leave, still shaking his head in disbelief, I jumped down from the counter. "Tim, before you leave, will you clean it up?"

In my version of this story, the animal in the foyer is a diseased possum or a raccoon (possibly rabid), and it's still warm. In Tim's version the animal is a "skinny ole rabbit" or "a little ole weasel," and it's been dead for days. In my version of the story, Tim is a little too eager to blow a hole through our floor. In his version I am standing on top of the kitchen counter, and I am screaming.

While my husband was in Illinois, my daughter and I went shopping for a while, and we returned home well after dark. As I opened the front door and started across the threshold, my daughter just two steps behind me, I heard music playing somewhere inside the house. "Did you leave your radio on?" I asked Emily.

"I don't think so," she said. I slammed the door and ordered her back into the car. Safely inside my car, the doors locked, I placed a frantic call on my car phone. (You guessed it.)

"Tim," I said, "I think someone might be in the house." Once again, click. Tim came in a run, carrying his shotgun like a wild mountain man tearing through the tree line.

"How do you know somebody's in there?" he asked breathlessly.

"The radio is on," I whispered. I saw a look pass across his face, but I figured he was just assessing the situation. We entered the house like dominoes. Emily was pressed to my back, and I was pressed to Tim's. "Do you hear the music?" I asked.

"Tim nodded. We started down the long hallway to the bedrooms. Tim stopped abruptly in front of the bathroom door, causing me to step on the back of his shoe and scrape the back of his heel. "Back up," he whispered.

Sorry," I whispered in return.

"You've about deboned my ankle," he said in a whisper, a very loud whisper.

"Shhhh!" Emily said. Again we started forward, and again Tim stopped dead in his tracks. I rammed my entire face into his back, mashing my lip on his shoulder blade.

"Ow," I said.

"I told you to back up!" he said out loud.

"Shhh!" Emily said, and again we moved down the hallway.

"I think my mouth is bleeding," I whispered.

"Good," Tim said.

"I mean it. I taste blood."

"Good."

"Really, you just about knocked my teeth out."

"Mom, please be quite," Emily said.

"Yeah," Tim said, "you are whining like I intentionally sucker punched you with my shoulder blade."

"Well," I continued in a hushed tone, "I just think you could show a little bit of concern since I just tore a hole in my lip."

"Hey!" Tim yelled, throwing his arms up in air, "if there's someone in this house, do me a favor. Come and get her."

"Tim!" I said softly. "He's going to hear you."

Tim, put his hands squarely on my shoulders. "Let me ask you a question. What kind of fool breaks into somebody's house and then turns on the radio?"

I couldn't really think of an answer.

"That about says it all," Tim said.

"You know, Mom," Emily said, "I kind of remember turning my radio on. I kind of remembered it in the car, but you'd already called Tim."

"So this creeping through the house thing has been for my benefit?" I asked.

"Uh, yeah, pretty much," they concurred.

When Tim tells this story, he simply walks through the house to reassure me. Of course, he's certain that there is no real danger from an intruder, because being an expert on hardened criminals and all, he knows for a fact that they don't usually listen to music while they steal your TV and VCR. When I tell the story, Tim's ankle is just barely bleeding, but I have a loose tooth. And when Tim opens Emily's bedroom door, he blasts her radio into bits.

As I turn out the lights and lock the doors, Norman Bates is lurking in every long shadow. I listen to the shifting of the house, to the phantom footsteps that sometimes stalk children in the dark. The wind is whistling a Hitchcock tune as every murderous tale rises from memory to walk the night. I lay the cordless phone near my pillow like a crucifix. Beware, you ghosts and goblins, you vampires and witches, you Norman Bates and Hannibal Lectors, all you creatures who go bump in the night. Beware! Another tall tale may be brewing on this spooky Sunday night, for the moon is bright and the dark is full of shadows, but my neighbor, Tim, is on call. And I know his number by heart.

★★★

Our lives are full of cloaked adventure, and superheroes live just next door. Sitcoms are penned from the dialogue of home and family. Foibles become the fodder for delightful stories. The recounting of tomfoolery is sacred, and Sabbath is the perfect campfire around which tall tales can be told.

Spend time with friends or family on this long and languid Sabbath day. Keep glasses full and snacks within reach. Then listen as the escapades of every day begin their ascent, as common ordeals are bedecked with significance, as life becomes legend.

# Sunday Dinner Menu

- Mini Pizzas
- Green Salad with Italian Dressing
- Simple Sugar Cookies and Ice Cream

## Mini Pizzas

### Ingredients

6–8 English muffins, split in half (Allow 2–3 halves per person served.)
1 (24-ounce) (720 g) can of tomato sauce or pizza sauce
16 ounces (450 g) of grated mozzarella
Grated Parmesan cheese
Olive oil
Garlic salt (optional)
Pizza toppings such as chopped pepperoni, bits of fried Italian sausage, sliced green or black olives, canned mushroom bits (drained), minced onion, and minced green pepper

### Preparation

Split English muffins in half, place on broiler pan, and brush with olive oil. Toast for 1 to 2 minutes under broiler or until lightly browned. Turn off broiler, and preheat oven to 450 degrees F.

On each toasted half, place 1 or 2 tablespoons of tomato or pizza sauce. Add pizza toppings. (For fun, you can have family members or guests put their own toppings on their mini pizzas.) Sprinkle lightly with garlic salt, if desired. Cover each half with mozzarella cheese, and sprinkle with Parmesan cheese.

Place on a cookie sheet. Bake at 450 degrees F (230 degrees C) for 5–10 minute or until cheese melts. For appetizers, cut each into six small wedges. Serve piping hot.

Serving size: 2 English muffin halves. (Approximately 240 calories for two halves of basic recipe. Calories will vary depending on selected toppings.)

Adapted from Mayme Pearson's "Mini Pizzas for Meals or Appetizers."

## Green Salad with Italian Dressing

### Ingredients

1 head of romaine lettuce, washed, dried, and torn into bite-size pieces
1 head of red leaf lettuce, washed, dried, and torn into bite-size pieces
1 cup (225 g) of diced tomatoes
1 medium red onion, halved and thinly sliced
8 ounces (225 g) of crumpled feta cheese
1 (4-ounce) (125 g) jar of sliced black olives
1/2 cup (125g) of grated Romano cheese
1 bottle of Italian dressing

### Preparation

Place the lettuce into a large bowl. Top with tomatoes, onion, feta cheese, black olives, and Romano cheese. Refrigerate until time to serve.

Prior to serving, add Italian dressing to taste, and toss well.

Serves 8. (Approximately 135 calories per serving; does not include dressing.)

From the kitchen of Paula Hartman.

# Simple Sugar Cookies and Ice Cream

## Ingredients

2 (8-ounce) (225 g) sticks of butter or margarine
2 cups (450 g) of sugar
2 eggs
1 teaspoon (4.6 g) of baking soda
1 teaspoon (4.6 g) of cream of tartar
4 cups (900 g) of flour
extra sugar for cookie topping

## Preparation

Cream butter and sugar. Add eggs. Mix in baking soda, cream of tartar, and flour. Mix and roll in balls, dip bottom of glass in sugar, and press down on ball of dough. Bake on ungreased cookie sheet at 325 degrees F (160 degrees C). Makes approximately three- dozen cookies.

Serving size: 1 cookie. (Approximately 187 calories per cookie.)

Adapted from Mayme Pearson's "Sugar Cookie

# SUNDAY #6

---

# A Friend in Sickness and in Health

Our pastor asks for prayer concerns and celebrations. An older woman, whose name I am unsure of, sitting in the back row, requests prayer for her husband, the gray-haired man who usually sits beside her. He is in the hospital on this rainy Sunday morning, recovering from a heart attack. Bobbie asks that we pray for her sister. She does not explain the reason, and no explanation is expected, because God knows after all. Kelly stands, and as she begins to speak, everyone smiles. Kelly always has an extensive list of prayer concerns, given in weekly installments like a Sunday morning soap opera.

Our pastor announces the birth of a baby girl to a young couple in our church. He does not yet know her name, only that she arrived safely, and as he begins to list others who are in the hospital, I think of my friend Barbara Jean.

Barb has not been feeling well lately. I won't go into great detail, but in the past month, she discovered a case of anemia requiring supplemental iron, an enlarged ovary resulting in an ultrasound, and a cystic cervix resulting in a biopsy (and it thankfully turned out to be benign). If that wasn't enough, this week she developed severe sinusitis and a painful bladder infection, requiring three new prescriptions and several boxes of super soft tissues.

This might finish a weaker woman, but not Barb. Barb is tough. She called me on Friday night. Her voice was raspy and deep. "You won't believe what happened to me today."

"What?" I asked.

"I haven't been eating very much, so my arms and my legs feel weak. As a matter of fact, everything feels weak. It took me forever to put my makeup on this morning. I actually had to lean against the sink for support. And you know what? When I walked out of the bathroom, Doug (her husband) had the nerve to say, 'Barb, you have mascara smeared under your right eye.' I must have given him a dirty look because he got really defensive and said, 'Barb, I just don't want you to go to work looking like a raccoon.' Can you believe he called me a raccoon?"

I smiled, imagining Doug's confused expression as I said, "So you went to work today?"

"I drove to the office, if you call that going to work. I mean, usually you have to make it into the building before you can officially call it going to work."

"Huh?"

"With all this rain we've been getting, the parking lot was a swamp. When I got out of the car, my weak feet just sort of took off without the rest of me, and I ended up doing this little Dorothy Hamel maneuver on just one foot through the mud. I fell and twisted my ankle. It hurt so bad I couldn't get up. I'd still be lying in the middle of the parking lot if one of my coworkers hadn't looked out the window and said, 'Hey, look, everybody. Barb is lying in the middle of the parking lot.'"

I tried to sound sympathetic, but I started to laugh. (We have been friends for a long time, so she is fully aware of my problem with inappropriate laughter.) "Then what happened?" I asked.

"They had to carry me into the office, and they about killed me doing it. Every part of my body that could get bumped got bumped. My boss had me fill out an accident report. I was really tempted to mention the knot I got on my forehead from being whacked against the doorjamb. I didn't, but only because my boss was being so sweet. She said, 'Barb, I want you to go back home and rest, okay?' I started crying, and I told her, 'I don't usually cry like this.' She said, 'I know.' Then she glanced down at the accident report I had filled out and laughed. Out loud. Know why?"

"Why?"

"Because I had written 8:30 in the spot marked 'Time of Death.' Do you think that's an omen?"

Again, trying to sound sympathetic while laughing, I said, "No, I just think you need more rest."

"Well you can just forget resting in this house. I might as well try napping in the middle of the expressway. After I drove myself all the way home, limped all the way into the house, limped all the way up the stairs to change out of my wet clothes, limped all the way back down the stairs to get an ice pack, and situated myself on the sofa, Buddy (Barb's eighty-five-pound golden retriever) began guffawing and wheezing. Then he puked on the living room carpet. You know how big Buddy is. Well, trust me. Everything he does is big. That was the biggest pile of puke I have ever seen. So I'm yelling, "Outside, Buddy! Outside!" as he keeps hacking and choking, and he pukes two more times. I had to clean it up. It was just awful."

I was now laughing in earnest. Having regained a bit of my composure, I asked, "What else could happen, Barb?'

"I'll tell you what else could happen. When my son got home from school and saw me on the couch with my foot propped on a pillow, he got worried. I'm not sure if he was worried about me or if he was worried that he might actually have to do something, but he went upstairs and called my mother. She's been here all evening. I told her, 'Mom, I'm fine. Go home.' She said, 'You're not fine, and I'm not going home until you are well.'" Her voice softened to a whisper. "My mother is never going to go home because I am never going to be well." We both start to laugh much harder than mere chuckling. The laughter was equivalent to dry heaves.

I stand and look out at the faces of the faithful as they bow their heads to pray, fragile people, like myself, who become ill and grow old, who bring casseroles of scalloped potatoes to those who are grieving, who write notes of encouragement to those who are struggling, who buy cans of tuna fish and peanut butter to feed those who are hungry, who most importantly, laugh. They laugh well. I met my friend Barbara Jean at this church. She laughs better than anyone else I know.

★★★

Life can be tough. It can be tough on everyone. There are no exceptions. If we don't cultivate our sense of humor, life will be even tougher. Learning to laugh is quite simply life's best defense. Those who laugh well embody the spirit of Sabbath, for while Sabbath teaches us what is important in life, it does so by reminding us not to take life or ourselves too seriously.

Laughter can be learned, but we must practice, practice, and practice. Fill this day with opportunities to laugh. Rent a funny movie. Listen to Bill Cosby. Find an old episode of *I Love Lucy*. Read Erma Bombeck. Call a friend who loves to laugh. Call a friend who thinks you are funny and talk away. Look through your high school yearbook. Play with a child. Better yet, play like a child. Life can sucker punch even the most robust among us. Learn to put up your dukes and fight back. Smile, chuckle, chortle, and guffaw. Roar!

*Paula Hartman*

## Sunday Dinner Menu

- Simple Seafood Soup with Crackers
- Cold Corn and Tomato Salad
- Mom's Corn Fritters
- Cranberry Salad with Lemon Dressing
- Lemon Dressing for Cranberry Salad

# Simple Seafood Soup with Crackers

(Chopped chicken breast and cream of chicken soup can be substituted for crab and cream mushroom soup.)

### Ingredients

2 (6-ounce) (360 g) cans of canned crabmeat
1 (15-ounce) (450 g) can of chicken and rice soup
1 (15-ounce) (450 g) can of cream of mushroom soup
1 soup can of milk
1 teaspoon (4.6 g) of paprika
Salt and pepper

### Preparation

In a saucepan, mix mushroom soup and milk. Add chicken and rice soup, crabmeat, and paprika. Salt and pepper to taste. Heat slowly, stirring often. Garnish with a little sprinkle of paprika, if desired.

Serves 8. (Approximately 283 calories per serving.)

Adapted from Mayme Pearson's "Simple Seafood Soup."

# Cold Corn and Tomato Salad

## Ingredients

2 (15-ounce) (450 g) cans of corn or kernels cut from 8–10 ears of
    cooked sweet corn
2 tomatoes, chopped
1 English cucumber, unpeeled, quartered and sliced
1 sweet onion, chopped
1 green pepper, chopped
1/2 cup (120 g) of red radishes, thinly sliced
1 bottle of Italian dressing

## Preparation

Drain canned corn or cut kernels from cooked corn. In a large bowl, place corn, tomatoes, cucumber, onion, green pepper, and radishes. Toss well. Add Italian dressing to taste. Chill for at least one hour.

Serves 6. (Basic recipe approximately 178 calories per serving. Total calories will depend on preferred salad dressing.)

From the kitchen of Paula Hartman.

# Mom's Corn Fritters

## Ingredients

1/2 cup (125 mL) of milk
2 cups (450 g) of corn cut from cob or 16 ounces (450 g) of canned corn
1 cup (225 g) of flour
1 cup (225 g) of cornmeal
1 teaspoon (4.6 g) of salt
2 teaspoons (9.2 g) of baking powder
1 egg
2 tablespoons (30 g) of finely chopped onion
Cooking oil

## Preparation

Beat milk and egg. Add corn and onion to egg mixture. Add dry ingredients alternately. Batter will be stiff. Drop by teaspoonful into a skillet with hot oil. Cook until browned. Turn the fritters over and cook until brown. Drain on paper towel to remove excess fat.

Makes approximately 12 fritters. (Approximately 130 calories per fritter; includes vegetable oil used for cooking.)

Adapted from Polly Hensley's recipe "Corn Fritters."

# Cranberry Salad with Lemon Dressing

## Ingredients

1 pound (450 g) of fresh cranberries
1 1/4 (360 g) cups of sugar
1 cup (250 mL) of water
1 (3-ounce) (90 g) box of lemon gelatin
1 cup (225 g) of raw apples, chopped
1 cup (225 g) of celery, chopped
1/2 cup (112 g) of walnuts

## Preparation

In a saucepan, place cranberries and sugar in water. Cook until cranberries are done. Add gelatin to cranberries while they are still hot. Stir until gelatin is dissolved. Cool.

In a serving bowl, place apple, celery, and walnuts. Mix. Add cranberry mixture, and blend. Chill for one hour.

# Lemon Dressing for Cranberry Salad

## Ingredients

1 cup (225 g) of sugar
2 beaten eggs
juice of one lemon
1/2 cup (125 mL) of water
frozen whipped cream, thawed

## Preparation

Place all ingredients, except whipped cream, in a saucepan, and mix well. Using a double boiler, bring mixture to a boil. Cook until thickened. Chill.

When ready to serve, add whipped cream to taste. Scoop on top of cranberry salad.

Serves 8. (Approximately 309 calories per serving; includes dressing and two tablespoons of whipped cream.)

Adapted from Mayme Pearson's "Cranberry Salad with Lemon Dressing."

# A Beginner's Guide to Playing with the Psalms

A dear friend of mine once said, "When you enter a place of worship, you should leave your baggage at the door and enter unburdened into timelessness." He spoke with a gentle sincerity, and I thought, *How profound and how totally impossible.* At least impossible for someone like me, a virtual black belt in the art of worry and rumination, a person whose mind tends to run in boundless circles around my every good intention, a person who not only enters the sanctuary with her baggage intact but tends to overpack as well.

The service of worship at our small church begins with an organ prelude during which the faithful are instructed to prepare their hearts and minds for worship. Our organist usually plays a familiar hymn appropriate for such preparation, and the dear souls who tolerate (and even encourage) my presence among them turn their thoughts to higher things. I, on the other hand, dig through my purse for a piece of chewing gum and write a quick check for the offering plate.

As our liturgist stands to read the call to worship, I begin to drift away, caught in an undertow of thought, tugged along the sandy bottom of my own mind by an irresistible current The opening hymn centers me. The responsive reading gives me the opportunity to whisper my plans for my afternoon to my husband without being noticed, restraining myself as our pastor reads his lines of liturgy, speaking quickly as the congregation reads their lines. (It's taken years of practice to perfect this syncopated dialogue.) It is only as our pastor begins to read the Scripture lesson that I am finally able to tuck my overnight case beneath the pew and settle into worship.

Our pastor is a slight man with a slight amount of hair. He has a gentle manner and an even voice, and at times he almost seems timid. But when he steps into the pulpit, he becomes reticently dynamic. His allure has little to do with a charisma and more to do with the quiet conviction with which he delivers his consistently sound message. He is living proof of the old adage "Still waters run deep."

In comparison to my pastor, who possesses an undercurrent of penetrating spiritual knowledge, I embody what might be called a babbling brook of belief. I have a tendency to talk too fast in language that is not always linear. I have an inclination to laugh at what others might consider inappropriate moments. And I have a reputation for expressing a slightly nontraditional attitude toward church doctrine, which the teenagers love and elders hope I will outgrow. To be honest, I think I make our pastor just a little nervous.

This morning our pastor is quoting a psalm attributed to the poet king, David. He recounts his own attempts to learn to pray the psalms and to even include in his practice less popular psalms that do not easily find their way into religious greeting cards. He adds that he finds it helpful to create titles for each psalm as a means of attaching them to specific life experiences. I barely hear the rest of his sermon. My mind bolts like a wild horse, unbridled and kicking up sod. I can barely wait to get home and personalize a few psalms.

I've been at it since lunch. I am nearly intoxicated by this exercise in biblical scholarship. I am sure this is how Tillich and all the great theologians felt as they delved into the truth of Scripture. Although I still have a great deal to do, I plan to illustrate my collection of personalized mini psalms and hand them down my children for posterity in an effort to guide them through the difficult times in life.

The first of my personalized mini psalms is taken from Psalm 3:7. "Rise up, O God! Deliver me, O my God! For you strike all my enemies on the cheek; you break the teeth of the wicked." It can be used to deal with a difficult coworker. I have titled it, "You'd Better Watch It, You Two-Faced Gossip Monger."

The next mini psalm in my growing collection is taken from Psalm 6:6. It offers help when dealing with a bad bout of PMS. "I am weary with my moaning. Every night I flood my bed with tears. I drench my couch with my weeping." I have titled it, "Poor, Poor, Pitiful Me."

The mini psalm I title, "Give Me Strength," is taken from Psalm 54:2–3, and the mother of any teenager who has told her to chill out can use it. "Hear my prayer, O God; give ear to the words of my mouth. For the insolent have risen against me."

This is my favorite so far. It is taken from Psalm 61:2. "From the end of the earth, I call to you when my heart is faint." I have titled it, "Searching for My Son's Floor." You can use it for fortitude when entering your son's room in search of scotch tape.

I am really on a roll. Our pastor was right. This feels great. When life is tough and full of frustration, I can let the psalmist speak for me, whine for me, gripe for me, wallow in self-pity for me, even demand retribution and vengeance on my behalf. I feel as though I could swing through the trees and beat my chest.

Then my daughter Emily enters the room and sits down beside me. I suddenly feel self-conscious, leaning forward to cover my creative endeavor. Seeing my Bible open to the book of Psalms and unaware that she is interrupting a penetrating spiritual epiphany, she casually flips the pages and points to Psalm 136. "That's my favorite psalm," she says.

I read the first line, "O give thanks to the Lord, for he is good, for his steadfast love endures forever." Knowing that she, too, heard our pastor's sermon, I ask, "What title would you give it?"

She thinks a moment and says, "Maybe something like 'My Psalm for All Occasions.'"

Why do I even take this child to church? So she can use her spiritual finesse to make me feel petty? The exercise is ruined, and now I am sulking. How can a person play with the psalms when there are so many blessings to count?

Maybe just living life is like praying the psalms. You experience happiness, anger, elation, and frustration. You rejoice, weep, exalt, and throw temper tantrums. You walk though valleys of despair and soar like an eagle. You learn to embrace the good with the bad and the sorrow with the joy. And if you hang in there, psalm by psalm, line by line, day by day, hour by hour, in the end you find yourself praying Psalm 150, "Let everything that has breath praise the Lord."

Hey, wait a minute. How did I end up here? I got up this morning, went to church, sang a hymn, listened to a sermon, demanded the psalms provide divine vindication for all my worries and frustrations, and then ended up feeling grateful for this average, ordinary life of mine.

I am calling our pastor. I have been tricked.

★★★

Everyone approaches worship in different ways. For some, the process is intellectual. There are concepts to be learned and doctrine to be comprehended. For some, the process is emotional. The hymns and liturgy tender a deep, often profound inner response. For others, worship is a social or corporate event. Worship creates community and fosters an environment of acceptance and encouragement. And for others, worship is a mystical experience. Within the sacraments of worship, the presence of the divine is encountered.

For some people, worship feels natural and easy. For other people, worship feels difficult and slightly off-key. Some find it moving. Some find it dry. Regardless of how we approach it and regardless of how we feel about it, worship possesses the ability to transform and renew. Regular worship syncopates life. It brings us continually to an encounter with the divine and keeps us is step with the Spirit's leading.

Create a place for regular worship in your life. Worship in the tradition of your ancestors, or strike a new path. Simply enter Sabbath time, baggage and all, just as you are. That is all you need to do. The spirit of Sabbath will greet you, take you into divine arms, and lift you into life.

## Sunday Dinner Menu

- Crock-Pot Pork Chops and Potato Dinner
- Onion Butter Biscuits
- Kentucky Walnut Pie

## Crock-Pot Pork Chop and Potato Dinner

### Ingredients

6–8 (3-ounce) (90 g) pork chops
1 (15-ounce) (450 g) can of diced potatoes, drained
1 (10-ounce) (300g) can of cream of mushroom soup
2 teaspoon (9.2 g) of paprika
Salt and pepper to taste
2 tablespoons (30 mL) of vegetable oil

### Preparation

In a skillet, heat oil on high. Place pork chops in hot oil. Season with salt and pepper to taste. Sear on both sides.

Spray the inside of Crock-Pot with cooking oil. Place pork chops into the bottom of the Crock-Pot. Place potatoes, mushroom soup, and paprika on top of pork chops. Mix lightly. Cook on high for 4 hours or on low for 8 hours. Serve potato mixture over pork chops.

Serves 6–8. (Approximately 258 calories per serving.)

From the kitchen of Paula Hartman.

*Paula Hartman*

# Onion Butter Biscuits

## Ingredients

1 package of onion soup mix
1 can of biscuits
3 tablespoons (45 g) of margarine

## Preparation

Preheat oven to 450 degrees F (230 degrees C).

Separate biscuits and place on a piece of wax paper or cutting board. Cut each of the biscuits into 4 pieces. Place cut biscuits pieces into a greased 5 × 9–inch pan or baking dish.

In a saucepan, melt margarine and blend in soup mix. Cover biscuit pieces with the melted margarine. Bake for 10 to 12 minutes or until biscuits are golden brown. Serve warm.

Serves 8. (Approximately 154 calories per biscuit.)

From the kitchen of Paula Hartman.

# Kentucky Walnut Pie (Pure Southern Decadence)

## Ingredients

8 ounces (225 g) of margarine, melted
3/4 cup (168 g) of sugar
1 cup (225 g) of walnuts
2 eggs
1/2 teaspoon (5 mL) of vanilla
9-inch (143 g) frozen pie shell

## Preparation

Preheat oven to 350 degrees F (180 degrees C).

Cream margarine, sugar, eggs, and vanilla. Add walnuts and chocolate bits and mix well. Pour into frozen pie shell. Bake for 30 minutes.

Serves 8. (Approximately 608 calories per serving.)

Adapted from Ida Bruner's "Kentucky Pie."

# SUNDAY #8

# Sing a Little Tune

I am no Mariah Carey, but I do love to sing. My only formal training took place in the backseat of a blue Chevrolet station wagon. I cut my vocal teeth on an eclectic mix of traditional hymns, folk music, cowboy ballads, and sea chanteys. My family's distinctive tribal music would accompany the passing scenery as we rode toward southern Kentucky, windows down and harmony in high gear. My dad, who was a trained tenor, sang the melody, and my mother, a natural soprano, sang harmony in voice as clear and lovely as fine crystal. My sister and I did the backup vocals. We were never really sure what my brother was doing. His inability to carry a tune often made it sound as though he might be singing something different than the rest of the family.

Once, while my brother was taking a bath, he began singing a wild medley of "This Little Light of Mine," "Jingle Bells," and the theme song from "Batman." My mother was standing in the hallway, listening and smiling as the passion of Pavarotti seeped from under the bathroom door. She put a finger to her lips as I joined in her eavesdropping, and she whispered. "Don't you ever tell your little brother that he can't sing. It might make him stop doing it, and that would be a shame." So it became a family secret, and my brother grew to manhood, singing fervently off-key in the backseat of our family car.

Although a little more melodic than my brother's, I did not inherit the incredible voices of either of my parents as my sister did. I have one of those voices I call a "filler-inner" voice. This means that I can carry a tune well enough to be warmly welcomed into a church choir and even be included in an occasional quartet but never really solicited for solo work.

My unimpressive voice bothered me a great deal when I was twelve and wanted nothing more than to sing with the Partridge family. It no longer concerns me these thirty years later because I have realized that any self-consciousness I might have concerning the quality of my mediocre voice pales in comparison to the joy I feel when I open my throat and sing.

True to my childhood training, I especially love to sing in the car. My car has the perfect acoustics for a Partridge family wannabe, and the radio is an added perk. Not only can I vocalize with my kids, but I can also sing with the true artistes of country and rock. Paul Simon and I have done remarkable duets. My Scottish brogue is second only to that of Lorena McKenna herself. I swear there have been times when Garth and I were so musically entwined that we nearly floated to heaven.

Including my children in these artistic endeavors has proved highly educational for all. My eighteen-year-old daughter knows the entire soundtrack of *The Best of Dean Martin*, and these are her exact words: "His voice alone could make you fall in love." Just yesterday I received a lesson in lyrics from my seventeen-year-old son, who shares my husband's passion for Leonard Skynard. "Give me back my woman," I sang.

"Mom, it's give me back my bullet," my son instructed.

"Are you sure?" I asked.

"Yeah, I used to think it was give me back my boogie," he explained. "But the name of the song is 'Saturday Night Special.' Thus, the bullets."

"Well, that does make more sense," I said, joining my son and Leonard in an exquisite trio, "Give me back … give me back my bullet."

I sing in the bathtub. I sing in the kitchen. I sing in the garden. I sing at work. When I'm singing, I can't worry or make lists. I can't ruminate or regret. When I sing, I enter an untroubled state where the angels carol, where little children dance with the divine, and where my departed relatives sing revival songs from a distant shore.

I sing when I'm tired. I sing when I'm lonely. I sing when the pain of living becomes so great that it threatens to shatter me like broken glass. I thought I might suffocate at my father's funeral; however, as I listened to the words of his favorite hymn, carried upon and within the voices of those who loved him, I began to breath, and finally, I began to sing.

I am singing this morning with my own congregation in my own little church. My daughter is standing beside me, singing in a soft soprano harmony that is as clear and sweet as fine crystal. It is a gift she inherited from her grandmother. The words to the hymn are simple. "I was created to praise you forever, created to praise you again and again." I lean forward and whisper into the ear of my friend Barbara Jean, "Barb, I want this sung at my funeral. And I want you to sing it, okay?"

She passes back a note written on an offering envelope. I says, "Is this something I should start rehearsing right away?"

My mom called one night not long before her last Christmas. "Your brother just called. He's singing a solo on Christmas Eve." (My brother is now a minister.)

"Mom, does he know can't carry a tune?" I asked.

"Nope," she said proudly.

My family was flawed, as most families are, but oh, how my family loved to sing. Singing redeemed us as we our opened our throats with passion, singing our way down every long road, sharing the privilege of doing it imperfectly.

★★★

Music is a healing force. It touches us at an emotional level and influences our character as individuals and as groups of people. Whether we sing, play instruments, tap our feet, snap our fingers, or bob our heads, music has the power to change us.

The right music can energize us. It can make us feel happy and restore our sense of hope and optimism. Singing, in particular, has been proven to boost our immune systems.

The bottom line is that we should always make time in our lives for music. In the words of Plato, "Music is a moral obligation. It gives soul to the universe, wings to the mind, flight to the imagination, and charm and gaiety to life and to everything."

Today, nourish yourself with a little music. Just relax and listen to a melody floating from the radio. Tickle the ivories, or take a shower and sing like you mean it. Let your spirit unwind. And once your soul is bobbing its head with abandon, the spirit of Sabbath will sing within you.

## Sunday Dinner Menu

- Tomato Soup with Crackers
- Tuna Olive Spread on Toast
- Chocolate Lush (for Special Occasions)

# Tomato Soup

### Ingredients

2 cups (500 mL) of tomato juice
2 cups (500 mL) of milk
3 tablespoons (45 g) of flour
3 tablespoons (45 g) of butter
1 1/2 teaspoons (7.5 g) of paprika
1 teaspoon (5 g) of salt

### Preparation

In a saucepan, add tomato juice into flour gradually. Cook on medium heat, stirring frequently, until thickened. Gradually add cold milk, stirring vigorously. Add salt, butter, and paprika. Stir until butter is melted. Serve hot.

Serves 6 with 6-ounce servings. (Approximately 120 calories per serving.)

Adapted from Mayme Pearson's "Tomato Soup."

# Tuna Olive Spread on Toast

## Ingredients

2 (12-ounce) (360 g) cans of light tuna packed in water
1 cup (225 g) chopped olives
2 tablespoons (30 g) grated onion
2 teaspoons (10 mL) of lemon juice
1/2 cup (120g) mayonnaise
8 slices of bread

## Preparation

Using a fork, mash tuna in a small bowl. Add chopped olives, onion, and lemon juice. Mix. Add mayonnaise to moisten. Serve on toasted bread.

Serves 8. (Approximately 258 calories per serving; includes 1 slice of bread.)

Adapted from Mayme Pearson's "Tuna Olive Spread."

# Chocolate Lush (for Special Occasions)

## Ingredients

1 cup (225 g) finely crushed graham crackers
8 ounces (225 g) margarine
4 ounces (120 g) chopped pecans
1 (8-ounce) (225 g) package of cream cheese
8 ounces (225 g) frozen whipped cream, thawed
1 cup (225 g) of powdered sugar
12 ounces (360 g) of semisweet chocolate
3 cups (750 mL) of 2 percent milk

## Preparation

Preheat oven to 350 degrees F (180 degrees C). Mix graham crackers, butter or margarine, and pecans.

Press into the bottom of a buttered 9 × 13–inch baking dish. Bake for 15 minutes at 350 degrees F (180 degrees C). Cool.

Beat cream cheese, whipped cream, and confectioner's sugar together. Spread on cooled crust.

Beat together instant chocolate pudding and 3 cups of milk. Spread over cream cheese mixture. Frost with whipped cream. Garnish with pecans.

Serves 10 with 6-ounce servings. (Approximately 431 calories per serving.)

Adapted from Edith Stein's "Chocolate Lush Dessert."

# SUNDAY #9

---

# It's All in How You Play the Game

The game board is on the table. We each have a soft drink and a rack of seven letters. The ceiling fan spinning above the table makes a soft clicking sound. We are concentrating, searching for words.

I can't explain what happens to me when I play this game, but I'm like a werewolf beneath a full moon. Normally I am not a terribly competitive person, but having seven scrambled letters in a little wooden rack awakens something animalistic in the marrow of my bones. I play this game as intently as Tiger Woods putts. When I win, I become as cocky as Muhammad Ali. I also fight dirty when my back is up against the wall. I will, without a single pang of guilt, make up a word, place the sequence of letters on the board, invent a contrived definition, and dare my opponent to challenge me.

The kids are playing with us tonight. My son turns D-E-N-T into S-T-U-D-E-N-T. He has improved. I think of the children when they were younger, sitting before the same game board. My daughter Emily would form one word from her letters, and she would refuse to remove a single letter from that word, passing again and again, passing up point after point until her one unique word could be placed into the mosaic of lettered tiles on the board.

My son, Mark, was just the opposite. He played impulsively, quickly playing any letters that would fit on the board. Most of his plays were two or three letter words, such as I-T, O-F, and S-E-T. We talk about

60

this as we play. Our teenagers laugh at who they used to be, not realizing that they are still very much the same.

"Do you ever spell ribbon with one B?" Emily asks. We shake our heads.

"Can you play robin?" my husband asks, demonstrating great generosity since he is lagging behind.

"Just put rib on the board," her brother tells her. "You are taking too long."

Finally, Emily places C–R–E–D–I–T on the board. She doesn't gain a lot of points, but it is a good word. She smiles at me, and I smile back. My husband and I have learned that we can no longer plan evenings like this, evenings when the children are home and relaxed, evenings when a board game is placed above other priorities. At sixteen and seventeen, an evening like this arrives as an unexpected gift.

I am looking at my rack—two E's, four N's, and a Z. I roll the letters in my head like a slot machine, searching, searching. I spot a lone P. I place P–E–N–N–E on the board. "It's a kind of macaroni," I tell my family.

"You totally made that up, Mom," my son says.

"Really," I reply. "It is a kind of macaroni." My son demands that I prove it. I do, not with the dictionary but with an actual box of penne pasta. I do not gloat, however. I am trying to remember if there is rule against using foreign words, and I am not sure if penne is a foreign word. There is no further challenge. I think I may have gotten away with something, and adrenaline surges into the core of my being. I feel a strange predatory howl rising in my chest. I know how the she–wolf feels when she has torn the throat from her prey. I am woman. I am beast. I am a wild beast of a woman.

My husband calmly places seven letters on the board. He plays C–O–N–Q–U–E–R on an open S. He earns a double word score and thirty-five extra points for playing all seven letters. I am stunned. It's a whole new game. The predator has become the prey.

The kids and I, now hopelessly behind, refuse to cower, refuse to give up. It's a fight to the finish. We will try to play every letter in our respective racks, every single letter. This is a matter of family tradition. This is a matter of honor.

Realizing that I can't play my Z, I hang my head in defeat. Emily and Mark sit before empty racks.

As we begin clearing the board, my husband writes, "The Winner", in large letters across his score and smiles. This is simple payback. His spouse pulled a similar stunt several nights prior, and as I recall, she might have also taken a victory lap around the table. We decide to play again. The racks are reset. The ceiling fan spins and clicks, and we are concentrating. Sabbath stretches like a contented cat, purring into the night.

★★★

Sabbath is a time for play, a time for double jumping, a time for moving kings and pawns, a time for buying houses and motels, a time for getting out of jail free, a time for sleuthing, a time for climbing ladders and sliding down shoots, a time for sinking battleships. At the game table, our minds focus on the task at hand as real time shifts to play time. Adults become children, and children become adults. We let the world spin without us for a little while.

Sometimes in the playing, we learn something unexpected about ourselves. We may even give our shadow selves room to breathe and move about. Today, find a worthy opponent, take out a game board, open it on the table, and toss the dice.

## Sunday Dinner Menu

- Granny's Everyday Meatloaf
- Sautéed Mushrooms
- Smashed Red Potatoes
- Pineapple Upside-Down Cake

---

## Granny's Everyday Meat Loaf

---

### Ingredients

2/3 cup (150 g) of dry bread crumbs
1/4 cup (60 mL) of 2 percent milk
1 1/2 pound (675 g) of lean ground beef
2 beaten eggs
1/4 cup (56 g) of grated onion
1 teaspoon (5 g) of salt
1/8 teaspoon (1.2 g) of pepper
1/2 teaspoon (2.5 g) of sage
1 (10 3/4-ounce) (322g) can of condensed tomato soup

### Preparation

In a large bowl, add 1/2 can of tomato soup and the rest of the ingredients. Mix well. Place in a 13 × 9 × 2–inch pan. Top with the other half of the tomato soup.

Bake at 350 degrees F (180 degrees C) for 1 hour.

Serves 8. (Approximately 243 calories per serving.)

Adapted from Ida Bruner's "Everyday Meat Loaf."

*Paula Hartman*

## Sautéed Mushrooms

### Ingredients

16 ounces (450 g) of fresh mushrooms
3 tablespoons (45 g) of flour
3 tablespoons (45 g) of margarine
salt and pepper

### Preparation

Wash and slice 16 ounces of fresh mushrooms. Place in bowl. Place flour in the bowl, and toss lightly through the mushrooms. In a large saucepan, melt butter. Place mushrooms into butter, and cover pan. Cook over low heat for 10-12 minutes, stirring occasionally. Add salt and pepper to taste.

Serves 6. (Approximately 81 calories per serving.)

From the kitchen of Paula Hartman.

# Smashed Red Potatoes

## Ingredients

12 red potatoes, small
1/4 cup (56 g) of margarine
1/4 cup (56 g) of sour cream
1/4 cup (60 mL) of milk (optional)
salt and pepper to taste
several strips of fried bacon, chopped, or bacon bits to garnish, if desired

## Preparation

Cook potatoes in lightly salted water until they are tender. Drain well.

Place potatoes in a mixing bowl. Using a potato masher, smash the potatoes roughly, leaving large lumps. Add butter or margarine and sour cream or yogurt. Blend. Thin with milk, if desired. Salt and pepper to taste. Garnish with chopped bacon or bacon bits.

Serves 10. (Approximately 235 per eight ounce serving; does not include bacon or bacon bits.)

From the kitchen of Paula Hartman.

# Mom's Pineapple Upside-Down Cake

## Ingredients

2 1/2 cups (562 g) of flour
1 1/2 cups (337 g) of sugar
2 1/2 teaspoons (11.5 g) of baking powder
1 1/2 teaspoons (6.9 g) salt
2 eggs
1 (8-ounce) (250 mL) can of sweet condensed milk
2 teaspoons of (9 mL) of vanilla
8 teaspoons of (40 g) of shortening
4 tablespoons (60 g) of margarine
1/4 cup (60 g) of brown sugar
1 20-ounce (600 g) can of pineapple rings in 100 percent pineapple juice

## Preparation

To make batter, cream shortening and eggs. Add sweet condensed milk and vanilla. Mix well. Add flour, sugar, baking powder, and salt. Mix for 2 minutes.

In a small saucepan, melt butter. Blend in brown sugar. Using a spatula, pour the brown sugar mixture into a lightly greased 8 × 12–inch baking pan. Place pineapple rings on brown sugar mixture. Pour cake batter over the pineapple.

Bake 50 minutes at 350 degrees F (180 degrees C) or until a toothpick placed in the center of the cake comes out clean.

Serves 10. (Approximately 441 calories per serving.)

Adapted from Polly Hensley's "Pineapple Upside-Down Cake."

# SUNDAY #10

---

# One Fish, Two Fish, Why Any Fish?

When I was young and naïve, very young and very naïve, I dreamed of marrying a farmer. This was probably the result of one too many brightly colored books about cute cartoon animals making cute animal sounds and having cute little animal adventures. Luckily, I did not tether my life to that of "farmer in the dell" before realizing that cows not only give milk. They also kick and produce copious amounts of manure. Roosters will chase you and flog you in the back of the leg, and cute little bunnies with droopy ears will bite you and make you bleed. Once I began to equate becoming a farmer's wife with getting a tetanus shot, I decided to marry Donny Osmond.

Maturity has shown me that when it comes to animals, I'm more of a zoo person. I like to watch animals swing, growl, and flap without cleaning up feathers, fur, or feces. I like to visit the animals and then go home. (It's sort of like being a grandparent.) Also, my ability to housebreak an animal is as intrinsic as my ability to play professional football.

In lieu of this, one of the ironic facts of my life is that I live in a house with a dog, two cats, two birds, a turtle, seven copper mollies, and fifty-seven snails. I have also managed to endure a tree frog, a lizard, two guinea pigs, Chinese fighting fish, a hamster, about half of a dozen hermit crabs, and at least a 150 goldfish in my tenure as a mother.

Perhaps, like poor Noah with his ark, this menagerie is part of my destiny. Maybe these creatures came into my life one by one and two by two and in sets of eight to teach me important lessons. Or perhaps I am endowing the presence of my furry, feathered, scaly housemates with far too much significance. I am really just a mother who can't say, "No! You cannot have a lizard!"

I've learned to feed our household pets so they do not starve. I've learned to bathe them so they do not infest my bed with fleas. I've learned to change their little box regularly so they do not use the carpet beneath my desk. I've learned to clean their cages so they do not pluck themselves to death. In short, I've adopted an attitude of humane tolerance, and I have actually learned to enjoy them; however, it has been a slow process.

Our cat, Zoey, the most senior of our mammalian populace, actually outdates my presence in my husband's life. When we were first married, Zoey would charge my leg, climb it by impaling my skin with her claws, and push herself off at my hip, taking flesh. She is very old now—a temperamental calico feline with arthritis and few remaining teeth. She's still convinced that she is queen. She strides through the house like a vintage prima donna wearing lipstick on her teeth and barking orders at the help.

One winter our neighbors, Tim and Noreen, decided it would be nice to have a barn cat. To kill barn mice, I suppose. As luck would have it, their little black and white barn cat did not really care for barn mice. One morning he discovered that our dog's pet door led to a place that we humans heated and that in this place we serve a delicacy called cat food in a can.

I made the mistake of feeding him—once. Every morning after that fateful feeding. I'd find him waiting at the cat dish. Soon I would wake to find him sitting on our bed, watching us sleep, waiting patiently for me to serve him breakfast. It did not take him long to figure out that sitting directly on my neck would get me up and moving ahead of schedule. Every morning after breakfast, I'd have one of the kids carry him home.

He was a laid-back cat, and my children loved him. I nicknamed our little vagabond "Hobo." This was another big mistake on my part. Naming an animal is the equivalent to signing adoption papers. So one morning after breakfast, he just stayed.

We acquired our birds the day before my sister moved to Colorado. She gave them to my daughter Emily. This was an outright act of sisterly retribution. My dear sibling cannot seem to forgive me for giving her sons two absolutely adorable guinea pigs. My kids no longer wanted them, and I assumed her boys, Julian and Britton, would enjoy them. I admit that I told her they were cute and tame and that they walked on little leashes because it was true. And I also admit I failed to mention that they voided little round balls at a rate three times their body weight and that they excreted the strongest ammonia known to humankind.

But did those two delightful balls of fluff ever wake her at 4:30 a.m. squawking SOS in parakeet Morse code to their un-caged comrades outside? Did they ever escape during their cage's weekly cleaning and fly wildly about the living room, slamming into the picture window? Did she ever attempt a frantic rescue mission while simultaneously fending off a black-and-white cat turned mountain lion? Did my little tokens of affection use the bathroom in their water? Or pull their feathers out? Or throw birdseed in a six-foot radius around their cages? I think not.

Now that Emily is away at school, BJ and Guildenstern, her blue and yellow parakeets (not to mention Cleo, her turtle) are my responsibility. Where are Fluffy and Rambo, the brown and white guinea pigs? My sister passed them along to some unsuspecting friend.

My aquarium and eight copper mollies were a birthday gift from my children. The fish arrived in a plastic bag, so we quickly filled the aquarium with ten-gallon jugs of water and transferred the fish into their new home. We christened them Snow White and the seven dwarfs. It was lovely. The fish were playing in an underwater garden of plastic plants and river rocks from the backyard.

When my sister called to wish me a happy birthday, I told her about setting up the aquarium. "You did what?" she gasped. "You need to let an aquarium sit for a couple of weeks before you add your fish. Their environment needs to stabilize! Don't be surprised if they all die."

When I told my daughter, her face fell. I reassured her, "Your aunt is making a big ordeal out of nothing. Remember the fuss she made because of those guinea pigs? These are cold-water fish, and this is cold water. Everything will be just fine." By the next morning, Sleepy and Doc were belly up.

I ran to the pet store and purchased enzymes to decrease the environmental stress the un-stabilized aquarium had placed on our little fish. I'm not sure what this liquid does, but I think it is the fish equivalent of Valium. We lost Sneezy the next morning. Dopey died two days later. The aquarium is stable now. It's been months since we had a toilet-side funeral, and our three newest mollies fit in with the originals.

Unfortunately, there has been an abundance of small snails in our pond. Thinking they would keep the aquarium clean, my husband and I plucked three snails from our pond and placed them into the aquarium. What we did not know is that snails breed to the ninth power of rabbits. Now they've given birth. It's a mess.

Sunday afternoon is leaning on Sunday evening. I've cleaned the turtle bowl, the litter box, and the birdcage. I worked nearly two hours, carefully straining gravel and rinsing plastic aquatic plants, removing at least fifty-seven infant snails from our aquarium. Our dog, Molly, and I took the baby snails along with two of the adult snails and returned them to the pond from whence they came. Molly, a seventy-five-pound ball of canine energy, jumped into the pond for a celebratory swim.

With my chores done, I settle on the couch to read a book about a man who whispers to horses. Molly finds a place on the floor to dry. It is then that I have to admit to myself that I love Molly's soft, black face and the way she tilts her head to the side when I talk to her. I love the way Zoë stretches out in the windowsill and flicks her tail in her sleep, dreaming of whatever cats dream about. I love the way Hobo curls up next to Molly like a purring puppy. I love the way Cloe hides beneath her plastic lily pad, contently camouflaged. I love the way BJ and Gildenstern sit close together on their perch like lovers. I love the way my fish play, chasing one another through the plastic fern.

My menagerie and I share an attachment born of tolerance. We share devotion rooted in tenacity. We share an understanding stoked by familiarity. We share a family that loves us in spite of ourselves. It's not perfect, but it works. In short, whether by chance or cosmic design, we share a place called home.

★★★

The book of Genesis tells us that the Creator made swarms of living creatures on the fifth day. The Creator made humankind on the sixth day. On day seven the Creator took time to rest, but our Creator probably had to get the menagerie fed, watered, and walked first. Care of the Creator's creatures must be done every day. Sabbath is no exception.

Sabbath creates the time to also enjoy these creatures. Spend some time today in the presence of an animal. Play with your dog. Stroke your cat. Give your hamster a fresh bed of cedar. If you don't own an animal, make a bird feeder, hang it outside, and watch for visitors. Visit a zoo. Find a stable, and go riding. Take a walk in the woods, and watch for deer and squirrels. By the Creator's hand, we are connected to all creatures, great and small. Sabbath celebrates that connection. So celebrate. Feed your fish.

*Paula Hartman*

## Sunday Dinner Menu

- Ham and Cheese Casserole
- Fried Yukon Gold Potatoes
- Breakfast Corn Bread
- Fried Apples with Vanilla Ice Cream

---

# Ham and Cheese Casserole

---

### Ingredients

1 (12-ounce) (360 g) package of precooked breakfast ham, chopped or
    cut into small pieces
8 slices of toasted bread, discard the crusts and cut into cubes
1 cup (225 g) of shredded cheddar cheese
1 1/2 (375 mL) cups of milk
6 large eggs
1 (14 1/2-ounce) (435 g) can of diced tomatoes, well drained
1 small (135 g) can of mushrooms, well drained
2 teaspoons (9.2 g) of paprika
1/2 teaspoon (2.3 g) of salt
1/4 teaspoon (1.2 g) of pepper
1/2 cup (120 g) of seasoned bread crumbs

### Preparation

Butter the bottom and sides of an 8 × 12–inch baking dish. Spread bread cubes evenly on bottom of pan.

In a bowl, beat eggs, milk, and paprika together. Add ham, tomatoes, mushrooms, and paprika, and mix. Pour egg mixture over bread. Sprinkle with seasoned bread crumbs. Cover and refrigerate for 8 hours or overnight.

Bake at 350 degrees F (180 degrees C) for approximately one hour until center is set. Remove from the oven and let sit for 15 minutes before serving.

Serves 8 with 1-cup servings. (Approximately 330 calories per serving.)

From the kitchen of Paula Hartman.

# Fried Yukon Gold Potatoes

## Ingredients

1 to 1 1/2 pounds (450 g–675 g) of Yukon gold potatoes, scrubbed, not peeled
2 teaspoons (10 g) of salt
1/4 cup (125 mL) of vegetable oil
2 tablespoons (30 g) of flour
1/2 small green pepper, chopped
1/2 small onion, chopped
2 tablespoons (30 mL) of olive oil
1 teaspoon (5 g) of paprika

## Preparation

Place potatoes into a large saucepan. Cover with water. Add salt. Bring to a boil. Cook until potatoes are tender. Drain. Allow potatoes to cool a bit. When cool enough to handle, cut potatoes into cubes.

In a small saucepan, sauté green pepper and onion in 2 tablespoons of olive oil until onion is translucent and the green pepper is tender.

Heat 1/4 cup of vegetable oil in a large skillet. Add cubed potatoes and flour to hot oil. Stir flour through the potatoes. Cook on medium heat, stirring occasionally, until potatoes are light brown and a little crispy.

When potatoes are done, add sautéed onion and pepper. Sprinkle with paprika. Stir into potatoes. Turn burner down to low, and cook for another 1–2 minutes. Place potatoes on a plate covered with paper towel to soak up excess oil. Place in a serving dish and serve hot.

Serves 8. (Approximately 295 calories per serving.)

From the kitchen of Paula Hartman.

# Breakfast Corn Bread

## Ingredients

1 1/2 cups (338 g) of yellow cornmeal
1/2 cup (120 g) of flour
1 tablespoon (14 g) of baking powder
1 teaspoon (4.6 g) of salt
1 teaspoon (4.6 g) of sugar
3 eggs
1 cup (250 mL) of milk
3 tablespoons (42 g) of butter (melted)
1/4 cup (56 g) of cream (optional)

## Preparation

Combine cornmeal, flour, baking powder, salt, and sugar in a large
bowl. Place the milk and eggs in a separate small bowl. Beat lightly. Add
liquid to cornmeal mixture, and beat batter until thoroughly blended.
Stir in melted butter and cream (if desired). Spread batter 1/2-inch thick
in a large shallow buttered baking dish.

Bake at 400 degrees F (230 degrees C) for 15–20 minutes or until well
browned. Serve hot with butter and jelly.

Serves 8. (Approximately 199 calories per piece; does not include cream.)

Adapted from Mayme Pearson's "Breakfast Corn Bread."

# Fried Apples with Vanilla Ice Cream

## Ingredients

1/2 stick (56 g) of butter or margarine
5–6 tart apples
1/2 cup (120 g) of sugar
1/2 teaspoons (2.3 g) of cinnamon

## Preparation

Peel apples. Remove cores and slice. In a medium-sized heavy skillet, melt butter. Add apples, sugar, and cinnamon. Cook until apple slices are tender. Add extra sugar to taste if apples seem a little too tart. Serve hot with a scoop of vanilla ice cream.

Serves 6. (Approximately 289 calories per serving.)

From the kitchen of Paula Hartman.

# Sunday #11

# A Hypochondriac Comes Clean

I am sick. Not sick as in chronic, serious, or terminal. I am sick as in just a head cold or just a little bug. I am beginning to fear that if I don't shape up, my family might have me put me to sleep. I am what nurses call a difficult patient. I refuse to stay in bed. In truth, I refuse to remain in a prone position of any kind. I prefer to shuffle pathetically through the house, to situate myself in a centrally located area, and to droop, cough, and blow my nose. I prefer to heroically wash dishes and do other household chores while cradling my forehead in my hand and sighing. Some might call this martyrdom. I call it making lemons into lemonade.

You see, I do not become ill often, and in the world of a healthy mom, I endure a constant barrage of people saying, "Honey, can you?" "Honey, will you?" "Mom, will you make me that thing I need?" "Mom will you take me?" "Mom, I forgot. I need seven dozen cookies by tomorrow." I seldom get to hear someone say, "Honey, why don't you just sleep in this morning," "Honey, go watch TV and let me clean the kitchen," "Mom, do you want me to get you a blanket?" or even, "Mom, why don't you take a nap before you bake the seven dozen cookies I need by tomorrow." Hearing words of familial concern is almost addictive. I have to work hard to not make it my drug of choice.

I'm afraid I make it difficult for others to take my illnesses seriously. I admit that I am a bit of a hypochondriac. Those closest people to me are aware of it. So is my doctor. There is nothing I can do about it. I believe I was born with this condition. When I was seven, a childhood playmate of mine died after a brief battle with a brain tumor. Terrified by the news of his death, I grew afraid that I, too, might get a brain tumor. This began the protective ritual of ending my nightly prayers by saying, "Let everyone I know live to be one hundred years old, and don't let me die from a brain tumor."

At eight, after watching a Tony Curtis movie about the magician Houdini, who died from a ruptured appendix, I began having a nightly attack of acute appendicitis. Night after night I'd sit in my father's lap as he tried to convince me that I only had a self-induced tummy ache, that my appendix was not going to burst in my sleep, and that I was not going to wake up dead.

When I was nine, my mother found a lump in her breast. It was surgically removed, and luckily, it was benign; however, it left an impression. At eleven I found a lump in my chest. In a state of hysteria, I ran to mother. She laughed and informed me that I simply needed a training bra.

At eighteen I began nursing school. I was given large textbooks to read, books with detailed descriptions of diseases as well as new and exotic maladies. Armed with new information, I stopped diagnosing only myself. I began diagnosing other people. I informed my father that because he tended to sweat a great deal, I was certain he was diabetic. He ignored my novice advice, apparently remembering the appendicitis ordeal. I also informed my mother that I was fairly certain she needed professional help for her obsessive-compulsive disorder. This did not go over well at all.

Just last year I lost a friend to lymphoma. Her first symptom was a bit of swelling above her collarbone. One day I noticed a slight bulge just behind my left collarbone. I showed it to my daughter Janell, who is a nurse, and she agreed. I went to my doctor and informed him that I was fairly certain I had lymphoma. He palpated my shoulders and my neck and stood back a bit to visually compare the difference between my left shoulder and my right, and then after a moment of thought, he asked, "Which shoulder do you carry your purse on?"

Imagine my relief at discovering that I have a well-developed scalene muscle, instead of a tumor requiring radiation and chemotherapy. This morning I said to my husband, "Honey, I'm just so tired, and my throat is so sore. What if I have mono? Maybe I should go to the doctor tomorrow."

Apparently recalling the lymphoma ordeal, my husband replied, "Why don't you just take it easy today and see how you feel tomorrow." His words were like music. I could almost hear angels singing.

I have known brave souls who have endured such physical challenges as cancer, open-heart surgery, and severe arthritis with silent stoicism. While I admire them for their courage, should I develop a serious malady of some kind, I will need ample pain medication. I will whine. I will get out of bed without assistance. I will ride my call button. I will fray the nurses' nerves. And my husband will be there with me, nodding sympathetically. He proves it each time I have a cold.

I inform my family that this cold might only be the tip of a medical iceberg, and compassionately, I crawl into my bed for a long nap. As I prepare to surrender myself to the sleep-inducing effect a cold tablet, I take a moment to thank my Creator for my normally healthy body, for the opportunity to rest and heal, for people who love me in sickness and in health. It is difficult to be ill. It would be more difficult if no one cared.

★★★

Sabbath is a divine balm for the wounds and weariness that afflict each of us, giving us divine permission to sleep, to rest, and to heal. Lack of sleep and the failure to truly rest can rob us of vitality, stamina, and optimism. Physical rest is not enough. We must allow ourselves to mentally relax as well, to let go of the guilt that often keeps our minds perched atop a to-do list even as our bodies are attempting to rest.

Today, take the time you need to really rest. Do something that relaxes your mind and your body. Take a long nap or actively rest by doing something so absorbing and enjoyable that your mind unwinds. When you feel restored, remember someone who is ill or someone who is simply weary from living. Be the spirit of Sabbath for them. Write an encouraging note. Make a phone call. Really listen. Visit. Take cookies to share or flowers to enjoy. Nod with sincere empathy. It may take a great deal to heal a broken body, but it often takes very little to nurture a weary soul.

## Sunday Dinner Menu

- Baked Chicken with Mushrooms and Noodles
- Broccoli Parmesan
- Waldorf Salad (No Mayo)

# Baked Chicken with Mushrooms and Noodles

## Ingredients

6 cooked chicken breasts, cut into small pieces
1/3 cup (83 mL) of olive oil
1 medium onion, chopped
1 clove of garlic, minced
1 cup (225 g) of sliced fresh mushrooms
2 cans of cream of chicken soup
1 soup can of 2 percent milk
1/2 teaspoon (2.3 g) of powdered thyme
1/4 teaspoon (1.2 g) of ground oregano
1/4 cup (56 g) of chopped parsley
1/4 teaspoon (1 g) of allspice
1 pinch of nutmeg
16 ounces (450 g) of dry noodles, cooked according to package directions

## Preparation

Heat olive oil in a medium-sized skillet. Heat oil on medium heat. Add onion. Sauté until translucent (3–4 minutes). Add garlic and cook one minute more. Add chicken and mushrooms. Cook until mushrooms are hot.

Add chicken to skillet.

In a mixing bowl, combine soup, milk, thyme, oregano, parsley, allspice, and nutmeg. Whisk together and pour mixture into the skillet with chicken. Cover and simmer slowly for 45 minutes to 1 hour. Stir occasionally. Serve over noodles.

Makes 8 servings. (Approximately 405 calories per 10-ounce serving; includes noodles.)

From the kitchen of Paula Hartman.

# Broccoli Parmesan

## Ingredients

2 bunches of fresh broccoli florets, cut about the width of a nickel (no stems)
1 teaspoon (4.6 g) of salt
3 tablespoons (45 mL) of olive oil
1/2 sweet onion, chopped
1 clove of garlic, minced
4 ounces (120 g) of shredded (not grated) parmesan cheese
1/4 teaspoon (1.2 g) of salt
1/8 teaspoon (0.5 g) of pepper

## Preparation

Place broccoli florets in a saucepan or cooking pan. Add 1 teaspoon of salt.

Bring water to a rolling boil. Boil for one to two minutes, and drain. (You can boil 3 or 4 more minutes if you like your broccoli a little tenderer.)

In a skillet, heat olive oil. When hot, add onion, and cook until tender. Add garlic, and cook for one additional minute.

Add broccoli florets, Parmesan cheese, salt, and pepper. Cook until well heated.

Serves 6. (Approximately 156 calories per 5 ounce serving.)

From the kitchen of Paula Hartman.

# Waldorf Salad (No Mayo)

## Ingredients

4 cups (900 g) of chopped apples
2 cups (450 g) of seedless grapes, sliced in half
2 stalks of celery, thinly sliced
1/2 cup (120 g) of chopped walnuts
1/2 cup (120 g) of frozen whipped cream, thawed
2 ounces (30 mL) of 100 percent pure frozen concentrate
Juice of one lemon
2 ounces (30 mL) of sweetened evaporated milk

## Preparation

In a serving dish, combine apples, grapes, celery, and walnuts. Mix well.

In a mixing bowl, add whipped cream, orange juice, lemon juice, and evaporated milk. Whisk together. If the dressing seems too thick, add a little more evaporated milk.

Add dressing to the apple mixture and chill.

You can also add other fruit to this salad, such as canned, well-drained mandarin oranges, pineapple, raisins, etc.

Serves 8. (Approximately 227 calories per 6 ounce serving.)

From the kitchen of Paula Hartman.

# SUNDAY #12

---

# Ninety Days to Great Cheeks

If you want to tighten your buttock muscles and firm the old gluteus maximus, you could purchase of video with the title *Butt Master: Ninety Days to Great Cheeks*. You could try aggressively yelling your way through a martial arts class, or you could become a marathon runner. All of these methods will work, given time. But if you really want to tighten and firm your derriere, climb into the passenger side of a car with a brand-new sixteen-year-old driver. As you do, deceive yourself into thinking you can remain calm. If you want rapid results, make sure the sixteen-year-old is someone you love more than anything else on the planet.

Teaching the older of my two daughters, Janell, to drive was frightening. She only wanted to drive at one speed—way too fast. I actually had a vivid nightmare in which we were driving down the road, picking off mailboxes. I had this dream because in reality this was how I felt when I was sitting in the passenger side of the car while my daughter was driving. She tended to cling to the right side of the road. It felt like we were missing mailboxes by mere millimeters. *Millimeters*, I tell you. After one particularly horrifying session of driving, I got out the car and said, "Listen, Miss Lead-Foot, if you don't slow down when I tell you to slow down, I am not riding with you anymore, and you can just get your license when you're are like, like thirty-seven."

To which she replied, "Mom, you need to relax. I have things under control."

The younger of my two daughters was her sister's antithesis. She also drove at one speed—about ten miles an hour. One afternoon after practicing for a little while in a large parking lot, I told her, "Now we are going to pull out into the street, and you have to try to drive at least near the speed limit."

She clutched the steering wheel and replied, "Mom! This steering wheel is a foreign object in my hands, and you act like I know what I am doing!" She actually ran a stop sign on the way to take her driver's exam.

My son was the easiest child to teach to drive, but he threw a wrench into the ordeal by trying to look cool while doing it. He wanted to drive with only his right wrist thrown across the steering wheel. He was also very concerned with having just the right music on the radio. He continually switched the radio stations, weaving occasionally, ever-so-slightly left of center. I finally turned off the radio and said, "Leave the radio alone, and keep your eyes on the road."

He just leaned back in his seat, driving with only his wrist across the steering wheel, and replied, "Mom, chill."

Fear is something we learn as babies when parents tuck us into bed and turn off the light, when we lie in the darkness, wondering if they are really ever going to return. This same fear becomes a consummate skill when we hand our keys to our children and then watch them skip or strut to the car, crank up the radio, and pull out of the drive. This fear does not really ease with time. At least it hasn't for me.

I have met some mothers who are able to do this with relative calm. I have noticed that these mothers usually have six or seven children, and I think they are really not in touch with reality anymore. Writer Anne Lammott says she believes that when a child is born, it comes out clutching one-fifth of its mother's brain in its hand. I believe her. I believe that if you have several children, it is sort of like getting a progressive lobotomy. That's why women with five or six children seem so calm.

I, on the other hand, still have two-fifths of my mind, so I can still panic with the best of them. In my defense, I have worked in the health care field for most of my adult life. I have seen a lot. The first death I ever witnessed was a nineteen-year-old child who fell asleep driving home from her fast-food job.

On Thursday nights our town's volunteer fire department tests its sirens. On a rational level, I know this, but on Thursday nights, if one of my children is out driving somewhere when the sirens go off, I feel a rush of terror, imagining them lying broken and bleeding, asking for their mother. I always glance at my husband for his reassuring "It's okay, honey" smile, but I never really relax until I see the car turn into the drive.

★★★

Some things that go bump in the night are very real, and some are just figments of our vivid imaginations. While fear is sometimes appropriate, it can also paralyze. Even as adults, we need to occasionally analyze the things we fear. We need to ask ourselves if our fear is an unexamined remnant from childhood. Does our fear arise from a past memory or wound? Is our fear keeping us from living our best lives? We also need to remind ourselves that fear is often the trade-off for the privilege of loving someone.

Sabbath allows time for this kind of reality check. The spirit of Sabbath will sit with us while we think things through. It will help us put irrational fear in check. With practice, Sabbath will teach us to recognize what our fear is trying to teach us. Take a little time today to think about what you fear. Ask yourself if fear is keeping you from recognizing happiness.

You don't need to search for something to ease you fear. Sabbath is not a time for judging, berating, or shaming your self for being afraid. Muster the courage to just sit with your fear for a short while. Then let it go and let the spirit of Sabbath work behind the scenes of your life. Tonight as you close your eyes to sleep, give sincere thanks for everything you have been given and for everything you have been spared.

# Sunday Dinner Menu

- Moist Baked Chicken
- Baked Sweet Potatoes
- Broiled Pineapple with Chocolate Sauce

## Moist Baked Chicken

### Ingredients

6 boneless chicken breasts, cooked and cut into small pieces
16 ounces (450 g) of sour cream
1/2 teaspoon (2.3 g) of garlic salt
1/4 teaspoon (1 g) of celery salt
2 teaspoons (10 mL) of lemon juice
2 teaspoons (10 mL) of Worcestershire sauce
1 cup (225 g) of fine cracker crumbs, divided
Paprika for garnish

### Preparation

Place chicken in a 9 × 13–inch baking pan. Sprinkle half of the bread crumbs over the chicken.

Mix sour cream, garlic salt, celery salt, lemon juice, and Worcestershire sauce in a bowl.

Pour the sour cream mixture over the chicken. Sprinkle the remaining bread crumbs.

Sprinkle with paprika. Bake at 300 degrees F (150 degrees C) for about an hour or until it is bubbly and the bread crumbs are browned.

Serves 6. (Approximately 307 calories per 6 ounce serving.)

Adapted from Polly Hensley's "Moist Baked Chicken."

# Baked Sweet Potatoes

## Ingredients

1 medium baked potato for each person
Olive oil
Margarine
Sour cream
Salt and pepper

## Preparation

Coat sweet potatoes with olive oil. Pierce each sweet potato several times with a fork or the tip of a sharp knife. Place the sweet potatoes on a rimmed baking sheet covered with aluminum foil. Bake at 400 degrees F (200 degrees C) for approximately 45 minutes or until potatoes are tender. Serve hot with margarine and sour cream. Salt and pepper to taste.

Serving size is one potato per person. (Approximately 303 calories; includes 1 tablespoon of margarine and 1 tablespoon of sour cream.)

From the kitchen of Paula Hartman.

# Broiled Pineapple with Chocolate Sauce

## Ingredients

1 fresh pineapple
chocolate ice cream topping

## Preparation

Turn oven on broil. Cut the pineapple in 1-inch slices. Place pineapple slices on a lightly oiled broiler pan. Place the broiler pan 4 inches from heat. Broil the pineapple for 4–5 minutes. Turn slices over, and broil for an additional 3–4 minutes.

Place warm pineapple on plate and drizzle each slice with 1 tablespoon of chocolate sauce.

Serving size is one slice of pineapple. (Approximately 80 calories per serving.)

From the kitchen of Paula Hartman.

# SUNDAY #13

---

# Purging the Clutter of a Lifetime

My sister is visiting, and we are sorting through an enormous stack of boxes in our barn. It seems an odd task for a Sunday, especially when we see each other so rarely; however, it needs to be done, and we both know it. For two hours my sister has been giving orders like a general, "Men, batten down the hatches! Throw that whole box away! Paula! What are you doing? You don't want that!" And I have been calmly obeying. This is simply how we work together. I think it is karmic payback.

My sister often—and I do mean often—tells a story about cleaning the basement, where we kept our toys and played when we were children. In her story I am nine, and I'm standing on the toy box. In the grand style of a Southern evangelist, I am quoting Holy Scripture and weeping about the poor children who have no toys, gnashing my teeth on the selfishness I see in my siblings, who are dawdling at the task of caring for the overabundance of toys in our possession. And in her story I am doing this while she and my brother do the actual cleaning. In her story she sweetly and tenderly suggests that we send some of our toys to poor, and I reply with by saying something like, "Clean, you pathetic sinner, clean!" I don't remember it that way.

Seven years ago we lost both of our parents. Mom had been sick for a long time with Lou Gehrig's disease. Dad had a massive heart attack just ten days after her funeral and died three months after her death. Still numb, we sorted the contents of their closets, cabinets, and drawers, discarding very little. Perhaps we were too tired and full of sorrow to make decisions. Perhaps we had endured too much at once. Perhaps everything felt too full of Mom and Dad. We took special items to our homes; the rest we packed into boxes. We covered the boxes with thick plastic, and we left them untouched, stacked like a cardboard mausoleum in the loft of our barn ... for seven years.

"Why did we save this?" my sister asks, holding up a rusted cookie sheet.

"Because it was Mom's," I answer, and she tosses it into the pile we have designated for throwaways.

"What were we thinking?" my sister says and laughs.

"Maybe it wasn't that rusty when we saved it," I reply.

"I never saw Mom use this," she says, holding up an object that resembles the odd love child of a corkscrew and shoehorn. "What is this?" We look at it, straining to remember.

"Toss it," we say together.

My sister pitches the mystery item into the pile we have designated for charity. "Maybe someone else will know what it is," she says. Pulling an orange and green crocheted comforter from the bottom of the box and making the same face she used to make when we were forced to eat liver and onions, she says, "This is disgusting."

In unison, we say, "Toss it."

"Do you want this? Could you use this? Do you think one of the kids would like this?" So the sorting goes. A slightly worn electric skillet, at least thirty-five generic cookbooks, an extensive collection of toile painted plaques, a family of collectible calico rabbits, a flock of collectable mallard ducks, and a stack of books are all deemed suitable for charity. Chipped vases, stained dish-towels, worn pot-holders, and stacks of old Christmas cards are discarded. We divide a box of crystals and cut glasses that were precious to our mother, and we each save a few pieces from a box of Christmas decorations.

We then turn our attention to four remaining boxes, which are full of our parents' photo albums. For most of the afternoon, we carefully peel photos from their pages. We scrutinize a box of old family pictures, debating identities. We laugh at old hairstyles, old boyfriends, and old husbands. There are photos that trigger forgotten pains, images that stir regrets, and we are silent as we study them, as silent as we would be standing before a coffin.

Before long we have a haphazard pile of unwanted pictures—endless duplicates, exhausting scenic shots, pictures that are blurred, pictures of strangers. We are keeping only the pictures we love. I look at my sister, her head bent as if in prayer, intently searching the photos in her lap. She looks a little wilted. It has been a long day. It has been a long seven years.

Tonight my husband will build a bonfire, and I will throw much that we have discarded into the flames. We will sit in lawn chairs and watch the fire turn all to ash. We will breathe the cool night air and watch the fire flicker. We will make s'mores with our children and try to keep them from torching one another's hair with flaming marshmallows. The fire will snap and weave in yellow blue. Our neighbors will join us, telling tall tales of West Virginia. My sister will retell her version of cleaning the basement, which I will deny.

My sister and I will sit with family and friends beneath a witnessing moon, aware that we are taking part in a silent ceremony, a ritual of letting go, and an unspoken reaffirmation of life and of family.

★★★

Sabbath is time for the clearing away of clutter. It allows time for the simple process of cleaning out a drawer, reordering a jumbled closet, or sifting through the chaos of our desk. Sabbath urges us to toss away of what is useless, impractical, worn out, and outgrown, to rid ourselves of pretentious and unloved clutter. It allows us to create new space for what is useful, needed, cherished, and adored. Sometimes as we rummage and sort through the mess we've collected in our dark corners and in our dusty boxes, we discover forgotten treasure.

Today, begin with one closet, a single drawer, or a solitary cabinet. Do not rush. Take the time you need to decide what is worth keeping, and then keep only that which you deem practical or loved and authentically you. As for the rest, open your hand, your mind, or your heart, and just let go. It's that simple.

## Sunday Dinner Menu

- Cabbage Casserole
- Mom's Buttermilk Corn Bread
- Orange Fluff

## Cabbage Casserole

### Ingredients

1 pound (450 g) of lean hamburger
1 small sweet onion, chopped
1 clove of garlic, minced
1 small head of cabbage, chopped
1 (14-ounce) (420 g) can of diced potatoes
3 cups (750 mL) of tomato juice
1/2 teaspoon (2.3 g) of celery seed
1 teaspoon (4.6 g) of paprika
2 tablespoons (30 mL) of olive oil
Salt and pepper

### Preparation

In a large skillet, fry hamburger. Drain grease. Add a little olive oil and the onion. Cook until onion begins to look translucent. Add garlic. Cook for about 5 minutes longer. Add cabbage, potatoes, celery seed, and paprika. Add a little more olive oil, if you like. Add 2 cups of tomato juice, and simmer until cabbage is tender. Add more tomato juice as needed. Add salt and pepper to taste. Serve warm.

Serves 8. (Approximately 206 calories per serving.)

From the kitchen of Paula Hartman.

# Mom's Buttermilk Corn Bread

## Ingredients

2 1/2 (562 g) cups of cornmeal
1 cup (225 g) of flour
2 teaspoons (9.2 g) of salt
1/2 teaspoon (2.3 g) of baking soda
2 teaspoons (9.2 g) of baking powder
1 cup (250 mL) of buttermilk, 1 percent milk fat
1 cup (250 mL) of 2 percent milk
2 large eggs
3 tablespoons (42 g) of melted margarine
2 tablespoons (28 g) of shortening

## Preparation

Preheat oven to 400 degrees F (200 degrees C). Place shortening in a cast-iron skillet or other heavy ovenproof pan. Place in oven. While you mix the corn bread batter, the shortening will melt, and the pan will become very hot. Doing this gives the corn bread a wonderful crust.

In a large bowl, mix cornmeal, flour, salt, baking soda, and baking powder. Mix well.

In large bowl, whisk together buttermilk, milk, eggs, and melted butter or margarine.

Add dry ingredients, and mix well.

Carefully remove the skillet or pan from the oven. Using a pastry brush or other small cooking brush, brush the melted shortening on sides of skillet or pan. Make sure the bottom of the pan is well covered. Pour corn bread batter into the hot skillet or pan. Reduce the oven's temperature to 350 degrees F (180 degrees C). Cook for 35–45 minutes.

The corn bread should be nicely browned. A toothpick place in center should come out clean.

After removing from the oven, allow corn bread to cool for about 5 minutes. Run a table knife around the sides of skillet or pan. Invert the corn bread onto serving plate. Be careful. The pan will still be very hot. Serve with butter or margarine, jelly, and/or honey.

Serves 8. (Approximately 138 calories per slice.)

Adapted from Polly Hensley's "Buttermilk Corn Bread."

## Orange Fluff

### Ingredients

1 (16-ounce) (450 g) container of thawed frozen whipped cream
2 (3 1/2-ounce) (105 g) boxes of orange gelatin
3 (4 1/2-ounce) (135 g) cans of mandarin oranges (drained)
1 (14 1/2-ounce) (435 g) can of crushed pineapple (well drained)
1–2 oranges for garnish

### Preparation

In a large mixing bowl, mix whipped cream, powdered gelatin, mandarin oranges, and crushed pineapple. Mix well. Pour into serving bowl, and chill. Garnish with orange slices around the rim of the bowl, if desired.

Adapted from my Aunt Shirley's recipe "Orange Fluff."

# The Singe and Scorch Method of Cooking

I take pride in the fact that I cook for my family almost every night. The definition of cook is "to prepare food for eating by means of heat." More often than I would like, the definition of my cooking turns into "to burn superficially" or "to shrivel with heat." Sadly, many of the meals I throw on the table involve the singe and scorch method of food preparation—at least on weeknights.

On weeknights *fast* is the operative word. Because I am a working mother and my children are busy teenagers, I usually have a mere twenty- to thirty-minute window of opportunity to execute what can only be called a pseudo-family dinner. The need for speed eliminates many if not most of our traditional family recipes. I have learned to substitute quickie versions of these meals. It is not the most satisfying way to cook, because the outcome is sometimes iffy.

Here is a typical quick to table menu: spaghetti with store-bought canned sauce, garlic bread, meatballs from the frozen food aisle, and bag-o-salad. Under ideal circumstances, I can pull this meal together in about twenty minutes, and it's fairly edible. Ideal conditions are rare. On most weeknights there are other factors at play. This is an example of what usually happens:

**4:00 p.m.**

I enter the front door of our home after my thirty-minute commute from work. My son is waiting at the top of the stairs. He tells me that he must leave at 4:45 sharp and that he has no clean underwear. I take off my jacket and proceed directly to the kitchen. I put water on to boil and prewarm the broiler.

**4:05 p.m.**

I gather laundry from three different bedrooms, run downstairs to the laundry room, place a load in the washer, and pick up the pile of my son's clean underwear from the folding table. As I return to the kitchen, the phone rings. I answer it and tell the person on the other end of the line that my son is in the shower.

**4:10 p.m.**

I put the spaghetti into the boiling water and the garlic bread into the oven. I feed the cats, who are playing follow the leader in and around my feet. The phone rings. I answer the phone and tell the person on the other end of line that my son is still in the shower.

**4:15 p.m.**

My son yells from the bathroom. He needs a towel. I find the linen closet empty. I run back downstairs to the laundry room, grab a stack of clean towels, and run upstairs. I give a towel to my son, whose wet hand is protruding from the bathroom door. As I turn to place the rest of the towels in the linen closet, the phone rings. I answer it, and I tell the person on the other end of line that my son is just getting out of the shower.

**4:20 p.m.**

I realize that the garlic bread is burning and that the spaghetti is four and half minutes past its optimal cooking time. I remove the garlic bread from the oven and locate the spaghetti strainer. The phone rings. I answer and notify my son that he has a phone call. I follow my son's directive to take a message. Now at seven and a half minutes past its optimal cooking time, I drain the water from the spaghetti.

**4:25 p.m.**

As I place the precooked meatballs into the microwave oven, my husband enters the kitchen. He wants to know the location of a small spring he left "right here."

**4:26 p.m.**

"What spring?" I ask as I cut open the bag-o-salad and dump the lettuce into salad bowls.

**4:27 p.m.**

My husband says, "It's about a fourth of an inch long. I left it right here a couple of weeks age." I note that he is pointing to the counter space between the coffeepot and the can opener. His face says, "I'm serious. I need it right now."

**4:28 p.m.**

I say to my husband, "Really, honey? You left a little tiny spring right there for two weeks. There's no telling where it is."

**4:29 p.m.**

My husband begins to search through kitchen cabinets and drawers. I take the meatballs from the microwave oven, open a jar of tomato sauce, pour it into a saucepan, and turn the burner on high.

**4:30 p.m.**

My daughter arrives home and begins a lengthy story that starts out, "You'll never believe what we're going to do." I fill plates with mushy spaghetti.

**4:32 p.m.**

My husband says, "Just tell me the truth. Did you throw it away?"

My daughter says, "Mom, you aren't even listening to me. What did I just say to you?"

**4:35 p.m.**

I call my family to the table.

**4:36 p.m.**

Everyone sits down. My son notes that the spaghetti looks a bit mushy. My daughter asks why the garlic bread is burned. I get up from my seat because there is no silverware on the table. I find the missing spring in the silverware drawer.

**4:40 p.m.**

My son gulps down his spaghetti, inhales several pieces of garlic bread, and excuses himself because he is running late for practice. My daughter leaves the table to start her homework. My husband feeds our dogs his last two meatballs. He must put the important little spring on the something or other. Immediately.

**5:00 p.m.**

I clear the table and start loading the dishes into the dishwasher. But I pause for just a moment to take a deep breath. I turn the radio on and remind myself that although our dinner was hectic and less than perfect, my children have never known real hunger. I kick off my shoes and remove my socks. Standing barefoot on the kitchen floor, I remember that no matter how mundane the chore or how simple the kitchen linoleum, I am blessed to be standing on holy ground.

★★★

Sabbath time seems to move at a slower pace. Windows of opportunity widen. There is time to make spaghetti sauce from fresh tomatoes and simmer it slowly. There is time to make bread from yeast or gravy from scratch. There is time to marinate meat, snap fresh green beans, and make dessert. These activities invite sampling, nibbling, and an easy conversation that continues through dinner.

The quickie meals of busy weekdays feed us, and they have their place; however, the slowly cooked, gently simmered meals of Sabbath nourish those who gather at the table long after the dishes are done.

Make a favorite dish or meal today. Take joy in the chopping and the dicing. Appreciate the miracle of bubbling, boiling, and simmering, the miracle of transforming food with heat. Then sit at the table and delight in what you have prepared with your own hands. When the meal is over, linger awhile. Simply enjoy.

# Sunday Dinner Menu

- Taco Salad
- Mexi-Thousand Island Dressing
- Refried Beans
- Easy Mexican Chocolate Cake
- Caramel Glaze

## Taco Salad

### Ingredients

2 pounds (900 g) of lean hamburger
1 medium onion, chopped
1/2 green pepper, chopped
2 (1-ounce) (30 g) packages of taco powder
1 1/2 cups (375 mL) of hot water
1 head of iceberg lettuce, torn or sliced
2 fresh tomatoes, chopped
Taco sauce
Sour cream
1 (14 1/2-ounce) (435 g) can of sliced black olives
1 (10-ounce) (282.5 g) bag of tortilla chips

### Preparation

In a skillet, fry hamburger, onion, and green onion until hamburger is well done and vegetables are tender. Add taco powder and water. Simmer slowly until water is absorbed.

On each plate, crush a layer of tortilla chips. Divide meat equally, placing it on top of tortilla chips. Follow this with a layer of lettuce. Top with tomatoes and black olives.

Serve with taco sauce, sour cream, and/or Mexi-Thousand Island Dressing.

Serves 8. (Approximately 228 calories per serving; includes 2 tablespoons of taco sauce and 2 tablespoons of sour cream per serving but does not include tortilla chips.)

From the kitchen of Paula Hartman.

# Mexi-Thousand Island Dressing

## Ingredients

1 bottle of Thousand Island dressing
1 (1-ounce) (28 g) package of taco powder

## Preparation

In a bowl, mix dressing and taco powder. Chill.

(Approximately 183 calories per 2 tablespoon serving.)

From the kitchen of Paula Hartman.

# Refried Beans

## Ingredients

2 (16-ounce) (450 g) cans of pinto beans, drained and rinsed
1 medium onion, chopped
2 cloves of garlic, chopped
2 tablespoons (30 mL) of olive oil
1 1/2 teaspoons (7 g) of cumin
1 1/2 teaspoons (7 g) of paprika
1/2 teaspoon (2.3 g) of chili powder
1 teaspoon (4.6 g) of salt or to taste
1/4 cup (62 g) of water (plus additional water, if needed)

## Preparation

In a saucepan, cook onions in olive oil until tender. Add garlic, and cook 1–2 minutes longer. Add pinto beans, cumin, paprika, chili powder, salt, and water. Cook on low for 20–25 minutes. Add additional water, as needed. Mash to desired consistency.

Serves 6. (Approximately 118 calories per 1/2-cup serving.)

From the kitchen of Paula Hartman.

# Easy Mexican Chocolate Cake

## Ingredients

1 box of devil's food cake mix
1/2 cup (375 g) of unsweetened applesauce
2 eggs
2 teaspoons (9.2 g) of cinnamon
1 teaspoon (4.6 g) of chili powder

## Preparation

Preheat oven to 350 degrees F (180 degrees C).

Add cinnamon and chili powder to dry cake mix. Add eggs and applesauce to the dry mix. Mix 2 minutes with electric mixer.

Pour batter into a greased a greased, floured 13 × 9–inch baking pan. Cook as directed by package instructions or until a toothpick inserted into center of cake comes out clean. Cool. Remove from pan.

# Caramel Glaze

## Ingredients

2 tablespoons (28 g) of margarine
1/2 cup (120 g) of firmly packed light brown sugar
2 tablespoons (30 mL) of 2 percent milk
1 teaspoon (4.6 g) of cinnamon
1 teaspoon (5 mL) of almond extract

## Preparation

Place all ingredients in a saucepan. Bring to a boil, and cook for 1 minute. Spoon the glaze over the cake.

Serves 8. (Approximately 278 calories per serving; includes glaze.)

From the kitchen of Paula Hartman.

# Sunday #15

# Practicing Self-Sabotage

I have had a week alone—no husband, no children. The week comes to an end today. In a few hours, my husband will return home from a business trip, and my children will return home from summer camp. As a result of this, I am feeling very dissatisfied with myself.

I had so many plans for this week alone. I had planned to do some serious self-evaluation. I planned work on a little spiritual renewal. I planned to work out every single day and be a few pounds lighter before everyone arrived home. I made a list. Looking back at the week, I wonder how I squandered so much time.

Monday, my day off, I slept almost all day, recovering from a long weekend at work. Plus I free from the usual beck and call of being a mother and a wife. I got up long enough to wander around the house, make plans to water the plants on Tuesday, eat a few chips, drink a diet soda, and go back to bed.

Tuesday was a workday. I was running late. I dashed downstairs to our laundry room to press a pair of work pants. I passed by the front door, and I opened it for our cat. He walked in and dropped what appeared to be a dead frog on the foyer floor. He then looked up at me as if to say, "What about that catch, babe?" Making a mental note to pick up the dead frog on my way back, I continued to the laundry room and quickly pressed my pants for work. As I ascended the stairs, the frog was gone. Gone. It's an unsolved mystery.

I felt a bit beat up after a busy day at work. I ate a small salad for dinner and fell asleep on the couch. At about three o'clock in the morning, I woke up with a spasm in my neck. I was drenched with premenopausal sweat, and I was starving. To remedy the situation, I ate some more chips (this time with a little chip dip), and I went to bed.

On Wednesday, I had a day off from work, so I wrote most of the day. To reward myself for my productivity at the keyboard, I had a cheeseburger for dinner, watched some television, and went to bed.

On Thursday, I worked. My son called just as I walked in our front door. He said that camp was going pretty well, mostly because there were a lot of cute girls there. He then went on to explain that he had been thinking about his life. He just wanted me to know that he planned to drink beer sometime in the near future. The conversation left me unsettled for most of the evening. I kept wondering, *Is this just a normal part of growing up? Am I failing as a mother? Does my son just tell me things like this to yank my chain?* I almost never went to sleep. I kept thinking, *There was actually a time in my life when I thought that I wanted children.*

Tonight I had planned to put on some good music, make a pot of coffee, and clean the house. But I was a little tired after working and not sleeping, so I took a long nap. Now I am watching the driveway for my family.

Have I mentioned any exercise? Have I mentioned any weight loss? Do I sound spiritually refreshed? No, no, and no.

Why do I set myself up for failure like this? To be honest, I do it all the time. I do it every single day I have off work. I always make unachievable lists, especially when I have time to myself. I should try making a realistic list like this:

1.  Stand in front of the refrigerator with the door open.
2.  Think about unloading the dishwasher.
3.  Hang up my bath towel.
4.  Find the remote control.
5.  Rest.

Having made a realistic list, maybe I could feel like I accomplished something. Like other busy women, I need to give myself permission to just rest. Rest is a need, not a luxury. When I have a day off or a week alone, without shame, rest should be at the top of my list.

★★★

Sabbath is not the time for making lists. It is not the time for setting unrealistic goals. It is not the time for pressuring oneself into accomplishing anything. It is a time for cutting one a little slack. It is a time for relaxing, for sleeping, for enjoying the people who care about you. Sabbath can restore your perspective and your sense of humor.

Today, for this one day, do not try to solve personal problems or the problems of the world. Give your mind and your body permission to relax and play. Pick up reins of your life on another day.

*Paula Hartman*

## Sunday Dinner Menu

- Cheddar Cheese Sandwiches on Rye Bread
- Pasta Salad
- Mississippi Cake with Frosting
- Icing for Mississippi Cake

---

# Cheddar Cheese Sandwiches on Rye Bread

---

### Ingredients

6–8 slices of rye bread
1 (4-ounce) (120 g) can of tomato paste
6–8 slices of cheddar
margarine

### Preparation

Spread margarine lightly on one side of bread. Place on broiler pan. Broil bread for about two minutes or until the bread is toasted. Flip the bread over. Spread tomato paste over each slice of bread, and a slice of cheddar cheese. Broil until light and bubbly.

Serving size: 1 sandwich. (Approximately 278 calories per serving.)

Adapted from Mayme Pearson's "Easy Open-Faced Cheddar Cheese Sandwiches."

# Pasta Salad

## Ingredients

6 cups (1.35 kg) of macaroni, cooked, enriched
1/2 cup (120 g) of chopped green pepper
1 cup (225 g) of chopped celery
1/4 cup (56 g) of finely chopped sweet onion
1 cup (225 g) of chopped cucumber
1 cup (225 g) of diced tomatoes
1 bottle of Italian dressing

## Preparation

Place the pasta, green pepper, celery, onion, and tomatoes into a serving bowl. Mix well. Add Italian dressing and mix. Chill for 1 hour before serving.

Serves 8. (Approximately 330 calories per serving.)

From the kitchen of Paula Hartman.

# Mississippi Cake with Frosting

## Ingredients

4 eggs
2 cups (900 g) of sugar
2 (8-ounce) (225 g) sticks of margarine, melted
1 1/2 (337.5 g) cups of flour
1 cup (225 g) of cocoa
1 teaspoon (4.6 g) of vanilla
1 cup (240 g) of chopped nuts
1 (7-ounce) (198 g) jar of marshmallow cream

## Preparation

Beat eggs and sugar until thick. Mix melted butter or margarine, flour, cocoa, and vanilla. Mix until batter is smooth. Fold the nuts into batter. Pour into a greased, floured 13 × 9–inch pan. Bake at 350 degrees F (180 degrees C) for 30 minutes. Remove and spread a jar of marshmallow cream on hot cake.

# Icing for Mississippi Cake

## Ingredients

1 (8-ounce (225 g) stick of margarine, softened
6 tablespoons (90 mL) of 2 percent milk
1 (16-ounce) (450 g) box of powdered sugar
1 teaspoon (5 mL) of vanilla
1/3 (150 g) cup of cocoa

## Preparation

In a medium saucepan, melt margarine. Add all ingredients and beat well. Remove from heat and spread over marshmallow cream.

Cut into 16 pieces.

Serves 16. (Approximately 662 calories per serving; includes frosting.)

Adapted from Rella Gaye Cogar's "Mississippi Cake with Frosting."

## SUNDAY #16

# Mother Talk

The thing I miss the most about my mother is her mother talk, the undercurrent of her continual fussing. All mothers do this in some form. It begins with unspoken fussing like adjusting her baby's blanket, dabbing at drool with a shirttail, checking to make sure that what she treasures most is still breathing.

As the child grows older, the fussing becomes a new monosyllable language of love. "No." "Hot." "Icky." Of course, the language deepens as the years pass. "Not before dinner." "Time for bed." "Stay in your own yard." "Don't go near the street." "Be careful." "You are not wearing that to school." "What did you do to your hair?" "Be home by midnight." On and on it goes, and a child learns to ignore it the way you learn to ignore a freight train barreling through your backyard. Still, it is always there, and the sound of it is comforting.

This morning I read a story in *LIFE* magazine about a mother who was seriously injured in the Oklahoma City bombing. Her children came close to facing life without her and without her mother talk. The mother's right eye was destroyed by the blast. When she arrived at her home, her left eye was swollen shut, so she could not see. Thankfully, the swelling decreased with time. Within just a few minutes of regaining her sight, she told her daughter, Sarah, "It's too cold to be wearing those shorts." How comforted Sarah must have been. At that moment, even though she was unaware of the significance of it, she had to have known in her heart that everything was going to be all right.

I remember the last conversation I had with my mother. It wasn't profound. My husband and I were planting a garden, our first attempt at gardening. I had called my dad to ask him how to plant my white half-runner beans. These southern string beans are a favorite of mine. Mom always had a pot simmering on the stove when came home to visit. When I would open my parents' front door, the distinct perfume of green beans and bacon grease was as satisfying as a hug.

Dad told me what I wanted to know, but Mom called back. She was afraid that I wasn't going to plant the beans properly. It was difficult to understand her because she was so very sick. She told me, "Paula, you need to put several beans together in a little mound of good soil. When they come up, put a stake in the mound so the plant can vine up. If you don't plant the beans right, you won't get a good crop." Little did I know, however, that it was the last mother talk I would ever hear.

My husband asked me this morning what he should let the kids get me for Mother's Day. I told him that it didn't matter. But in my heart I had only one real wish on that Mother's Day. I wanted to pick up the phone and hear Mom fuss at me about anything—anything at all.

As I contemplate a more tangible Mother's Day gift, my son sits down beside my husband and asks, "Mom, can I go to Billy Joe's house for dinner?"

Before I can answer, my husband says, "No. It's Mother's Day. We are going out for dinner, and you are not wearing that." Oh, the beautiful sound of father talk. My son looks a little irritated right now, but someday he will miss it.

★★★

We all have memories, some good and some bad. Sometimes when we allow ourselves a little downtime, those memories will arrive like uninvited houseguests who show up unexpectedly and who plan to spend the entire day. Our memories may include people who love us and who are dear to us, but just as often they can include people who aggravate and embarrass us, people who give us unsolicited advice and unrequested opinions, and people who fuss and worry us to death, mostly out fear that we will not survive without them.

A memory might induce feelings of nostalgia, homesickness, or sentimentality. On the other hand, memory has a way of triggering feelings of regret, grief, heartache, or even anger. It can make us smile or ruin our day. The spirit of Sabbath implores us to embrace the feelings associated with a memory without allowing the feelings to highjack our day.

If an unpleasant memory arrives on your day of Sabbath time, do not let it begin a rumination of self-judgment. Greet it with wisdom. Be thankful for what the memory taught you. Greet it with a sense of humor. Find the hilarity in just being human. And gently send it on its way.

Then return to the present moment. Be thankful that you are alive with time remaining to live life fully. Feel at peace with your past and with your past selves. Allow yourself to be thankful for the imperfect person you are today. There is only one of you. Give yourself a hug and seize the day. Seize the day with gratitude and joy.

## Sunday Dinner Menu

- Chicken Vegetable Soup
- Salad with Aunt Mayme's Unusual Thousand Island Dressing
- Salad with Aunt Mayme's Usual Thousand Island Dressing
- Grandma McCoy's Sheet Cake
- Topping for Grandma McCoy's Sheet Cake

# Chicken Vegetable Soup

## Ingredients

3 cups (675 g) of cooked chicken, white meat, roasted
1/2 chopped onion
1 large bulb of minced garlic
1/2 chopped green pepper
1 cup (225 g) of fresh corn
1 cup (225 g) of fresh green beans
1 cup (225 g) of fresh sliced carrots
1 cup (225 g) of chopped potatoes, peeled
2 (16-ounce) (500 mL) containers of chicken broth
2 teaspoons (9.2 g) of paprika
2 teaspoons (9.2 g) of celery seed

## Preparation

In a large Dutch oven, kettle, or Crock-Pot, add chicken, onion, garlic, chopped or canned vegetables, paprika, and celery seed.

Cover with chicken broth. Bring soup to a boil, and then lower to a healthy simmer. Cook on stove, stirring occasionally for 2 hours or until fresh vegetables are soft and flavors are blended. Add additional chicken broth as needed. Add salt and pepper to taste.

If you are making this in a Crock-Pot, cook on high for four hours, stirring occasionally. Add chicken broth as needed. Add salt and pepper to taste.

Serves 6. (Approximately 312 calories per serving.)

From the kitchen of Paula Hartman.

---

# Salad with Aunt Mayme's Unusual Thousand Island Dressing

---

## Ingredients

4 tablespoons (56 g) of mayonnaise
4 tablespoons (56 g) of chili sauce
1 small onion, diced
12 stuffed olives, chopped
2 hard-boiled eggs, chopped

## Preparation

Mix and serve over lettuce wedges or favorite salad greens.

Serves 6. (Approximately 77 calories per serving.)

Adapted from Mayme Pearson's "Unusual Thousand Island Dressing."

# Salad with Aunt Mayme's Usual Thousand Island Dressing

## Ingredients

1 cup (225 g) of mayonnaise
3 tablespoons (13.8 g) of catsup
2 tablespoons (9.2 g) of chopped celery
2 tablespoons (9.2 g) of sweet pickle relish
1/2 teaspoon (2.3 g) cayenne pepper (optional)

## Preparation

Mix ingredients, chill, and serve over lettuce wedges or favorite salad greens.

Serves 6. (Approximately 167 calories per serving.)

Adapted from Mayme Pearson's "Thousand Island Dressing."

# Grandma McCoy's Sheet Cake

## Ingredients

1 stick (240 g) of butter or margarine
1/4 cup (60 g) of shortening
4 tablespoons (56 g) of cocoa
1 cup (250 mL) of water
1 cup (250 mL) of buttermilk
1 teaspoon (4.6 g) of baking soda
2 eggs
1 teaspoon (5 mL) of vanilla
1 teaspoon (4.6 g) of cinnamon
2 cups (450 g) of flour
2 cups (450 g) of sugar

## Preparation

Place sugar and flour in a large mixing bowl. Blend and set aside.

On stovetop in a large saucepan, bring butter or margarine, shortening, cocoa, and water to boil. Add mixture to dry ingredients and mix well.

Add buttermilk, baking soda, eggs, vanilla, and cinnamon. Mix well and pour into a greased sheet cake pan. Bake 20 minutes at 400 degrees F (200 degrees C).

# Topping for Grandma McCoy's Sheet Cake

## Ingredients

4 ounces (120 g) of margarine, melted
4 tablespoons (56 g) of cocoa
1 (16-ounce) (480 g) box of confectioner's sugar
6 tablespoons (90 mL) of 2 percent milk
1 tablespoon (15 mL) of vanilla
1 cup (225 g) of crushed pecans, if desired

## Preparation

Place the confectioner's sugar and cocoa into a mixing bowl. Add melted margarine and vanilla. Add 6 tablespoons of milk. Mix well. If necessary, add additional milk until the topping is the desired consistency. Fold in pecans, if desired.

Spread icing while cake is still hot. Cut in 16 pieces.

Serves 16. (Approximately 338 calories per serving; includes icing and pecans.)

Adapted from Rella Gaye Cogar's "Grandma McCoy's Sheet Cake.

# Sunday #17

# Living in Paradise

"Mom, he's hilarious," my daughter says, looking through the window, watching the man of our house swimming on a hot Sunday afternoon. She's referring to the fact that her father, a full-grown man, is doing his own version of cannonballs in an overgrown wading pool. "I'm getting my camera," she says.

The summer heat today is excruciating. In spite of our ceiling fans, which are oscillating at full speed, the humidity wafting through the open windows has dampened everything in our house without air-conditioning. It has been this hot and humid most of the summer.

Although I would have preferred central air or even a few air-conditioning units, the heat finally compelled my husband to buy a fifteen-foot-wide, four-and-a-half-foot-high swimming pool for our backyard. He worked for days removing a circle of sod from the backyard. He then shoveled bags and bags of sand onto the bare soil. He smoothed the sand and spent hours lying on the grass, eying his level and smoothing the sand again and again until the spot was perfect. The only thing my husband does halfway is the dishes.

Finally, when the pool area had been prepared, my husband pulled and tugged on a coil of rigid siding, an enormous blue plastic liner and a pump, wrestling them into position. The water truck arrived two days later, filling the little pool with gallons of ice-cold water. You could still hear the crunching of the truck's tires on our gravel drive as my husband climbed the shaky aluminum ladder and splashed in. "How's it feel?" I asked, standing outside the pool, running my fingertips through the icy water.

"G-g-g-reat," he said, smiling through his blue lips. "C-c-c-ome in."

"I think I'll wait until it warms up a little," I say.

"Mom, you have to see this," my son says, pulling me from my weeding to the back of the house. Peering around the corner like spies, we watch the man who normally does the responsible work of fathering and husbanding. He begins to circle the pool like a great white shark and then bends into a perfect forty-eight-inch surface dive. When he finally surfaces and stands, I realize he is wearing a pair of bright green goggles. "We should buy him some flippers?" my son grins.

Later the grinning boy will join the goggled man in the little pool, where they will play aqua wrestling and do handstands as my daughter snaps covert photos through the kitchen window.

As the day grows longer and hotter, my daughter finally succumbs to the lure of chlorine wafting through the kitchen window. Amused, I watch as she carefully climbs the aluminum ladder. She is carrying a six and a half foot inflated raft complete with a backrest and a beverage holder. My husband comes through the back door. "Emily wants a glass of iced tea." He looks through the window and smiles.

The afternoon wanes, and the moon appears. It is large and full of orange. I ease myself into the pool. My husband, his hair wet and slicked back, smiles as I bounce, breathing in little gasps, attempting to adjust to the cool water. I can read his mind, and so I threaten, "If you dunk me, I'm getting out." He smiles again, and we swim quietly in the moonlight.

Surfacing beside me, he plants a kiss on my mouth and says, "I think we live in paradise." And this is why I love my husband.

★★★

Sabbath strengthens our imagination because it sets time aside for play. Play enhances our capacity for optimism and fortifies our sense of humor. It wakens a childlike sense of fun that others find irresistible. Sabbath time provides time for an unrestrained surrender to the childlike wonder that still sees the potential in a cardboard box or a bottle of bubbles.

This kind of imaginative play does not involve technology. It requires the stuff of an uncomplicated childhood—a Hula-Hoop, a badminton set, a basketball, a box of crayons, a model car kit, modeling clay, jacks, or sidewalk chalk. The potential ingredients of simple play are endless and inexpensive. The difficult part of play is giving ourselves permission to do it.

Today, avoid technology and take a little time to recall how you played as a child. If this requires a quick trip to the dollar store, go and then just play. You will feel younger and happier when you are done. Without even trying, you will carry this joy with you as you return to your more adult activities. And don't be surprised if you find yourself starting a water fight while doing the dinner dishes. Fight with laughter and abandon.

The spirit of Sabbath implores us to play. And if you are playing with a friend or family member, play nice.

## Sunday Dinner Menu

- Meatballs for Subs
- Sub sandwiches
- Sweet and Sour Veggie Salad
- Frozen Yogurt Pie

## Meatballs for Subs

### Ingredients

2 pounds (900 g) of lean ground beef
2 beaten eggs, beaten
1 cup (225 g) unsweetened applesauce
1 large onion, chopped
1 cup (225 g) of bread crumbs
2 teaspoons (9.2 g) of salt
1 teaspoon (4.6 g) of pepper
14 ounces (420 g) of pizza sauce
1 cup (250 mL) of water

### Preparation

In a bowl, mix ground beef, egg, applesauce, onion, breadcrumbs, salt and pepper. Mix well. Form the meat mixture into small balls.

Place the meatballs into a large skillet on medium heat. Brown them on all sides. When brown, add catsup and water to the skillet. Cover and simmer for 20–40 minutes.

See the following instructions for preparing sub sandwiches.

---

# Sub Sandwiches

---

## Ingredients

8 whole-wheat hoagie buns
8 ounces (240 g) of mozzarella cheese

## Preparation

Open hoagie buns and spread lightly with butter or margarine. Place buns under broiler for 1–2 minutes or until buns are lightly browned. Remove from oven. Turn off broiler and reset oven to 350 degrees F (180 degrees C).

Place several tablespoons of pizza sauce on one side of each bun. Place 6–8 meatballs on top of the pizza sauce. You can add a little more pizza sauce to each sub, if desired. Cover with mozzarella cheese. Close subs. Wrap each one in tinfoil. Place in oven for about 15 minutes at 350 degrees F (180 degrees C). Serve hot.

Serves 8. (Approximately 490 calories per sub; includes bun.)

Adapted from Mayme Pearson's, "Swedish Meatballs via Kentucky."

# Sweet and Sour Veggie Salad

## Ingredients

1 cup (225 g) of cauliflower florets
1 cup (225 g) of broccoli florets
1 cup (225 g) of shredded cabbage
1/2 cup (120 g) of celery, sliced or chopped
1/2 cup (120 g) of chopped green pepper
1/2 cup (120 g) of chopped red or orange pepper
1/2 cup (120 g) of chopped onion
1/4 cup (60 g) of thinly sliced radishes
1/4 cup (60 mL) of wine vinegar
1/2 cup (120 g) of apple cider vinegar
1/4 cup (60 g) of sugar
3 tablespoons (45 mL) of olive oil
1 teaspoon (4.6 g) of salt
1/2 teaspoon (2.5 g) of celery seed

## Preparation

Put cauliflower, broccoli, cabbage, celery, peppers, onion, and radishes into a large serving bowl. Mix well. Place in the refrigerator until dressing is ready.

In a saucepan, place vinegars, sugar, oil, salt, and celery seed. Cook on medium until ingredients are blended and the sugar has dissolved. Chill.

When vinegar dressing is cold, add to vegetables and mix well. Serve cold.

Serves 6. (Approximately 117 calories per serving.)

Adapted from Betty Ritter's recipe "Sour Vegetable Salad."

# Frozen Yogurt Pie

Note that you can make this dessert using any fresh or frozen fruit you want. Just pair the fruit with a comparable yogurt. For example, pair sliced bananas with banana cream yogurt. I love blueberry, but there is plenty of room for creativity with this recipe.

## Ingredients

1 1/2 cups (350 g) of fresh or frozen blueberries
1 (12-ounce) (360 g) container of frozen whipped cream, thawed
1 (6-ounce) (180g) container of blueberry yogurt
1 premade graham cracker crust

## Preparation

In a bowl, mix whipped cream and yogurt. Mix well. Fold in blueberries. Using a spatula, put fruit mixture into the graham cracker crust. Cover with plastic wrap and freeze.

Serves 8. (Approximately 198 calories per serving.)

From the kitchen of Paula Hartman.

# SUNDAY #18

# The Beauty of Crayons

Our pastor is talking about grace. I am sure he is making profound parallels between Scripture and everyday life, but this particular morning finds me unable to concentrate. My mind is full of movement and unbridled thought. I shift uneasily on the pew. I watch the light from the stained glass windows paint patterns of light onto the floor. I look up at the arched, wooden ceiling and watch the ceiling fans whirl in silent circles. The candle flames are also restless.

Too young to appreciate the pastor's sermon, a young girl named Miriah colors a picture of Noah and his ark. Miriah is wearing a red dress like the alter vestments and her blonde hair falls softly across her face as she concentrates. I watch her carefully select a crayon. Her tongue is protruding from her small lips, moving like the candle's flame. A black-and-white elephant blushes lavender beneath her hand. Our pastor's voice rises in pitch as if to gain my attention, but I cannot take my eyes away from Miriah, longing to stretch out on the pew to help her work.

Finally home, my husband and I stretch out on the sofa to read the newspaper. As I turn the pages, I keep thinking of Miriah's crayons. I recall the smell of them. I remember the long summer afternoons spent at my great aunt's house. She was my father's aunt, and she did not own a working television. A little bored, my sister and I would drink ginger ale and listen to the conversation of the adults.

Sensing our restlessness, our aunt would give us a stack of blank paper and a can of well-used crayons. Inhaling the perfumed muse of colored wax, we would dream the afternoon away, lost in the creation of multicolored characters, imaginary places, and make-believe adventures.

Impulsively, I put aside the paper along with all the grown-up things of this day—the book I planned to read, the menu I planned to compile, the coupons I planned to clip. Instead I open a drawer in my dresser and take out my own box of ninety-six perfectly sharp crayons, a recent gift from my daughter, who seems to understand her mother better than most. I inhale the incense of first grade. After locating a pad of paper, I move outside to the picnic table and begin to draw. I create a tree full of late summer—raw sienna and forest green with a garden fence laced with vines and flowers, shamrock and purple mountain majesty. I begin to relax and breathe.

My daughter finds me, taking her own sheet of paper from the tablet. We talk about college. A true artist, Emily begins to draw a butterfly with elaborate wings of blizzard blue, plum, and wild strawberry. I marvel at how bold she has become, how grown up she looks with the sun playing in her hair. I wonder what I will do when she leaves in the fall and her room is empty for weeks at a time. I begin to draw a little house into my picture.

Emily looks up and asks, "What color are you going to make your house?"

"I haven't decided," I answer. I remember the difficult time my mother had letting go and of the pain it caused her children. Looking at this beautiful child, dreaming her canvas of color, I hope for the courage to let go gracefully. Knowing she will always have a place to return, I make my house "tickle me pink" with a winding path of "marvelous" and a door of "unmellow yellow."

★★★

Sabbath allows us room to dream and re-dream the canvas of our lives. It persuades us to let our imaginations play hopscotch upon our lists and obligations. It inspires us as we rethink the way we perceive our world. Sabbath playfully dares us to color outside the lines, to select colors outside our normal color palette, and to create with no pressure.

Today, find a quiet place and a medium to help you reimagine reality and to reimagine yourself. Use colored pencils, chalk, watercolor paint, or a simple box of crayons. Spread out. Make a glorious mess if you feel like it. Press lightly, or press hard. Refuse to follow the rules. Let the spirit of Sabbath give you permission to dream and to remember who you were, who you are, and who you will be.

## Sunday Dinner Menu

- Chicken Paprikash with Rice or Noodles
- Cauliflower Salad with Rice or Noodles
- Dressing for Cauliflower Salad
- Something Very Fine

---

## Chicken Paprikash with Rice or Noodles

---

### Ingredients

5 cups (1.125 kg) of cooked chicken, white meat, roasted
1/2 cup (120 g) of chopped onion
2 tablespoons (28 g) of paprika
2 tablespoons (30 mL) of olive oil
1 (8-ounce) (240g) container of sour cream

### Preparation

Heat olive oil in a large skillet. Add onions and cook until tender, about 5 minutes. Add cooked chicken and paprika. Simmer on low until chicken is hot. Add sour cream. Mix until smooth. Simmer until hot. Serve over rice or buttered noodles. (Use approximately 3 tablespoons of margarine.)

Serves 6. (Approximately 529 calories per serving; includes 1 cup of buttered noodles.)

Adapted from Polly Hensley's "Chicken Paprikash."

# Cauliflower Salad with Rice or Noodles

## Ingredients

1 head of cauliflower
1 head of lettuce or greens of your choice
1 purple onion
1 (10-ounce) (300 g) package of frozen peas
3 tablespoons (42 g) of bacon bits

## Preparation

Break cauliflower and lettuce or greens into bite-size pieces. Slice onion very thin. Boil the peas until tender. Drain and rinse with cold water. Dice bacon and fry until crisp. Place all ingredients in large serving bowl.

Add dressing and toss well.

# Dressing for Cauliflower Salad

## Ingredients

1 cup (225 g) of mayonnaise
1/3 cup (75 g) of Parmesan cheese
2 tablespoons (28 g) of sugar

## Preparation

Blend all ingredients in a small bowl. Spread dressing on salad like you would a cake. Refrigerate overnight.

Serves 6. (Approximately 274 calories; includes dressing.)

Adapted from Polly Hensley's "Cauliflower Salad."

---
## Something Very Fine
---

## Ingredients

1 (3 1/2-ounce) (105 g) box of lemon gelatin
1 (13 1/2-ounce) (450 g) can of crushed unsweetened pineapple, drained
    well (save juice)
1 pint (900 g) of frozen whipped cream, thawed
1/2 cup (120 g) of chopped walnuts

## Preparation

Bring reserved pineapple juice to a boil. Place the lemon gelatin into
a serving dish. Cover gelatin with boiling pineapple juice. Stir for 2
minutes until gelatin is completely dissolved. Place in refrigerator until
slightly thickened.

When gelatin begins to thicken, add whipped cream, pineapple, and
nuts. Refrigerate. Serve cold.

Serves 6. (Approximately 147 calories per serving.)

Adapted from my great-grandma Mary Bell Hensley's, "Something
Very Fine"

# SUNDAY #19

---

# An Exhausted Mother's Shakespearean Moment

This has been one of the most trying weekends of my entire life. I am running a bath. As I watch the water fill the tub, I consider drowning myself.

Our son, who had extensive knee surgery on Wednesday and who is recuperating in the overstuffed recliner in our downstairs den, is the reason for this Shakespearean moment. "To be or not to be? Is it better to suffer the verbal jabs and demands of a temperamental child or to hurl my naked forty-one-year-old body into the white porcelain abyss before me?" Weighing the options, death by peppermint does not sound all that unpleasant.

I remind myself that he is in a great deal of pain, that his pain medicine is making him irritable, and that neither he nor I have been sleeping well. This does not erase the reality of the past four day— delivering ice packs, giving pain medication, changing video games, returning ice packs to the freezer, preparing trays of food, filling water glasses. It does not erase the reality of the two weeks ahead of me. The doctor said, "You'll have two tough weeks." Was he looking at my son, or was he looking at me? It's all a blur now.

In addition to playing video games while he convalesces, my son has developed an obsession with his socks. I can't tell if he is merely having hot and cold flashes in his feet, or if he is simply playing a cruel game to test my maternal loyalty. He demands that I remove the sock from his foot, the one below his injured knee. The entire time I am trying to pull it gently from his size-nine foot, he yells, "Mom, you are killing me. Why don't you try to be just a little rougher?" Ten minutes later he tells me that his foot is cold and that he wants his sock back on. Again, he yells. Ten minutes later his foot is hot, and he wants the sock off again. I am beginning to feel like one of those test mice who, when given continual mild shocks of electricity to test the effect of stress, curls into a furry little ball of rigor mortise.

In between video games, during the rare moments when his feet are maintaining a constant temperature, Mark practices a newly honed vocal maneuver. He opens his throat and bellows, "Ma-a-a-a-a!" in a clear nasal tone as ear-shattering and unnerving as a fifth-grader, blowing her brand-new saxophone directly into your face! "Ma-a-a-a! I need an ice pack." "Ma-a-a-a-a! I need my socks off." "Ma-a-a-a! You are killing me." "Ma-a-a-a! Do we have anything to snack on?" "Ma-a-a-a! These chips are going to make me puke." "Ma-a-a-a. Ma-a-a-a. Ma-a-a-a. Ma-a-a-a." It may just be the fatigue, but he's beginning to sound like a flock of rabid sheep.

I managed to escape this ordeal for one hour this morning to attend church. I left a detailed list of instructions with my husband, offering to take my cell phone in case he needed me. My husband just smiled the smile he always smiles when he thinks I'm being silly, sipped his coffee, and told me to enjoy the service. I took my cell phone anyway. Apparently, I am the only one who fully understands the intensity of the situation.

Our pastor, a father of three, began his children's sermon with what I am sure he meant to be a little playfulness. Using a set of finger puppets that his five-year-old daughter made in Sunday school, he demonstrated the conflict between Moses and Pharaoh. He began smashing his costumed index-finger Moses into his costumed index-finger Pharaoh, and with each blow, he said, "Let my people go! Let my people go!"

The faithful seemed to enjoy our pastor's comedic effort, rewarding him with laughter. But not this exhausted mother. Suddenly, I was ringside, watching a biblical battle of epic proportion. Not only did I want the finger puppet Moses to crush the thin head of the finger puppet Pharaoh, but I also wanted him to shred Pharaoh's little papyrus body into confetti. I had to restrain myself to keep from shouting, "Come on, Moses! Pulverize him!"

I took a deep breath and managed to regain my composure. I tried to concentrate on the rest of the children's sermon, savoring the calm of the sanctuary. I actually began to feel a little better. Then Pastor Phil began his pastoral prayer. Kneeling at the altar rail, he requested mercy for the homeless, compassion for the downtrodden, relief for the poor, and courage for the terminally ill. He then invited us to offer a personal prayer or to simply reflect during a time of silence. He did not know that he had inadvertently given an unbalanced woman in his congregation permission to reflect on her precarious mental and emotional state. Big mistake. Big. But the deed was done.

I began to weep like a spoiled child on the shoulder of the Almighty, one who obviously had a few pressing things to take care of. Pastor Phil had just finished bringing them to divine attention. I didn't care. Silently, I prayed, "Please. Please. Please (sniff) fix my son's knee (sniff). If the fixing is going to take (sniff) like a long time (little choking gasp), send help ... or send (large choking gasp) sedatives and not for him, for me!"

I'm not sure, but my sobbing may have been audible. And I may have been banging my forehead against the pew in front of me. I say this because the people sitting around me stopped praying for the homeless, the downtrodden, and the terminally ill, long enough to pass tissues back, over, and down the pew. I left the sanctuary with a headache.

My husband was reading the Sunday paper as I walked in our front door. The house was quiet. He was still sipping coffee, and he looked far too relaxed. Then, as if on cue, "Ma-a-a-a-a!" yelled my son from the overstuffed recliner downstairs. His shouting has now taken on a maniacal quality that is frightening our cat.

Finally, Jenna arrives. Jenna is my son's girlfriend, a petite girl with brown hair and a sweet face. I meet her at the door. "I'm glad you're here," I whisper.

"Ma-a-a-a-a!" I feel my right eye twitching.

"You can relax for a while. I can handle him," Jenna says as she descends the stairs to lion's den, undaunted.

Do I wait to see if she has things under control? No, I do not. I run for the bathtub, and after a moment of Shakespearean angst, I submerge my weary body into warm peppermint. I drift to a place where there are no socks, a place where the whole world goes barefoot. I listen to the sound water makes when your ears are deep beneath it. I listen to the beating of my own heart. I drain the tub only when I have become gloriously shriveled. I emerge from my porcelain oasis, feeling a little more refreshed and a little less suicidal.

I walk to the top of the stairs. Strangely, I hear nothing. I wait for a few seconds. Still, I hear nothing, nothing at all. She's killed him! I'm certain of it. How could I have been so selfish? I dawdled around too long in the bathroom, and now a sweet, innocent girl has committed murder. Frantically, I try to think of a way to dispose of the body.

I descend the stairs slowly for the 145 time today, preparing myself to face my son's lifeless body lying in the overstuffed recliner, one sock on and one sock off. "Hi, Mom," my son says in his natural voice like a normal person, like the son I usually cherish.

To my surprise, Jenna is sitting on the floor with her bare foot in Mark's lap, and he is struggling to put her sock on her foot. "Ouch! Ouch! You're killing me! Killing me, I tell you!" she yelps as my son tries to maneuver the sock over her toes. "See how hard it is," she tells him. "Now imagine putting it on your big, fat foot." Jenna is laughing, and my son is laughing too. And I know there is hope.

★★★

At times the grit and grime of life will literally thrive on our best intentions and devour our carefully laid plans, seeping in like a fungus, consuming neglected corners, tarnishing what shines, rusting that which is exposed. The strain of life can rob us of much-needed rest and leave us emotionally on edge. Even caring for those we love immeasurably can exact a toll. There are times when the required care seems to leave no room for a sabbatical.

Pockets of Sabbath time set aside for self-care and sequestered from the chaos of even the most trying of times can offer a much-needed retreat, a welcomed nurturing of mind, soul, and body. Compassionate self–care lessens the wear and tear that can leave us feeling irritable and resentful.

The spirit of Sabbath mandates the tender self-care we all require to mend and thrive. Sabbath time restores the stamina we need to once again face life's challenges head-on with hope and humor. Today, take good care of yourself. Loaf, luxuriate, and linger. Don't forget to ask for help when you need it, and if necessary, go straight to the top.

## Sunday Dinner Menu

- Baked Fish with Sauce
- Figaro Sauce for Fish
- Squash and Onion Sauté
- Blackberry Pudding

# Baked Fish with Sauce

## Ingredients

8 fillets of mild fish, such as cod or catfish
4 tablespoons (56 g) of melted margarine
1 tablespoon (15 mL) of lemon juice
1 tablespoon of (15 mL) of lime juice
1/2 teaspoon (2.3 g) of salt
1/2 teaspoon (2.3 g) of paprika

## Preparation

Preheat oven to 350 degrees F (180 degrees C). Grease a rectangular baking pan. Cut fish fillets into desired servings. Place fish skin side down in the pan.

Mix melted margarine, lemon juice, lime juice, salt, and paprika. Drizzle over fish. Bake uncovered for 15–20 minutes until fish flakes easily with a fork. Remove from oven. Dress hot fish with Figaro sauce, and serve.

# Figaro Sauce for Fish

## Ingredients

2 hard-boiled eggs, chopped
1 teaspoon (4.6 g) of chopped chives
1 teaspoon (4.6 g) of chopped dill pickle
1 teaspoon (4.6 g) of dry mustard
Dash of Worcestershire sauce
3/4 cup (168 g) of mayonnaise
2 tablespoons (28 g) of catsup
Salt and pepper

## Preparation

Mix well. Refrigerate until ready to use. Serve over baked fish.

Serves 8. (Approximately 234 calories per fillet; includes sauce.)

Adapted from Mayme Pearson's "Baked Fish with Figaro Sauce."

# Squash and Onion Sauté'

## Ingredients

3–4 small yellow squash, chopped into cubes
1 medium onion, chopped
1/4 cup (62 mL) of olive oil
1/2 cup (120 g) of cornmeal
Salt and pepper to taste

## Preparation

In a cast-iron skillet or other heavy skillet, heat olive oil. When hot, add squash and onion. Turn heat down to medium. Add cornmeal and mix. Cook on medium, flipping the cubes of squash over frequently. You can add a little more olive oil, if desired. When the cornmeal begins to brown, turn the heat down to low and continue cooking, stirring often until squash is fork tender and cornmeal is brown.

Serve hot.

Serves 6. (Approximately 175 calories per serving.)

From the kitchen of Paula Hartman.

---
# Blackberry Pudding
---

## Ingredients

8 ounces (240 g) of melted margarine
1 cup (225 g) of sugar
1 cup (225 g) of flour
1/2 cup (125 mL) of 2 percent milk
1 (14-ounce) (420 g) can of blackberries

## Preparation

Preheat oven to 350 degrees F (180 degrees C).

In a mixing bowl, cream margarine and sugar. Add flour and mix. Add enough milk to the dough to make it the consistency of cake batter.

Place dough in a well-greased 8 × 8–inch baking pan. Pour the blackberries over the dough.

Bake for 25 minutes or until golden brown. Serve with a scoop of vanilla ice cream.

Serves 8. (Approximately 513 calories per serving; includes one scoop of vanilla ice cream.)

# SUNDAY #20

---

# The Ominous Truth about Fireflies

I know there are people who have never seen snow, people who have never shoveled snow from their driveways, and people who have never been hit in the back of the head or squarely in the face by an ice ball. They live in tropical forests or near Miami Beach and have great tans all year-round.

But this I did not know until recently. There are also people who have never seen fireflies, people who have never chased a blinking star across a summer lawn, people who have never held a spark of lightning in the tunnel of their hand. These people live in Colorado, and one of them is married to my sister.

"Jim saw his very first lightning bug when he and Leanne were here," I tell my husband as we walk along the garden's edge at dusk. The grass is a reflection of the night sky, full of glitter and twinkling. The summer has been wet, a little too wet. Our tomato plants are yellow and slim, each bearing the weight of only one or two small tomatoes; a powdery mildew destroyed our pumpkin plants. Our beans are growing, but the vines, climbing from the muddy, clay soil, look frail. The grape arbor and the lilac bush are molding. The only things that are thriving in this damp yard are the marigolds and the fireflies.

"It must be too dry in Colorado," my husband says.

"It's kind of sad," I say, recalling the relaxed summer evenings I spent in pursuit of blinking bugs. My mom would supply their temporary prison, a canning jar complete with a carpet of grass and a hole-studded

143

lid. One by one, I would follow their fitful flight, giving chase along the shadowed fence line, reaching into the burning bush, crawling beneath the blue spruce. I would hold them lightly in my hand as I placed them into my jar. I would fall to sleep watching them. After I fell asleep, my dad would release the prisoners, allowing them to fly away, winking into the night.

My friend Filly was never allowed to catch lightning bugs as a little girl. Her mother would not allow it because fireflies apparently relish gourmet meals of slugs and aphids, so they would keep the wheat clean.

"We lived in northern Ohio, not exactly the wheat belt." Filly laughs as she tells me this. "Kids are so gullible."

I spent this Sunday afternoon in the hammock, reading a gardening magazine, searching for a solution to our moldy summer garden, and finding instead an article about lightning bugs. For this reason, tonight I watch the weaving and darting of light across the lawn with renewed interest, thinking of my poor brother-in-law. I ask, "Honey, did you know there are 124 different species of fireflies in North America?"

"But none in Colorado," my husband replies.

"Nope," I say. The crickets are chirping in short sporadic crescendos from the locust trees. An occasional bullfrog *bur-umps* from the pond. "Do you want to know something really amazing?" I ask my husband. "The fireflies out in the open are all male, and their flashing is really flirting. They're really just showing off."

"Hmm," my husband says.

"Yes," I continue. "The female firefly sits on a leave and or a twig. When a potential mate comes blinking by, she flashes her tail to signal him. When he lands, they mate."

"Hmm," my husband says.

"I'm not even to the amazing part yet. Every species of firefly blinks in a unique pattern. Some of the female fireflies learn to imitate the flashing of another species. That way they can lure a foreign male to their leaf and then eat him when he lands.

"Hmm," my husband says.

"It's called aggressive mimicry," I tell him.

"Hmm," my husband says.

Later, still fascinated by this new bit of knowledge, I call my friend Barb. When I tell her about the firefly femme fatales, she says, "And I thought all that blinking was just innocent fun. Now it seems downright sinister, doesn't it?" Then we laugh.

"It's called aggressive mimicry," I say.

"I'll try to remember that," she vows. She humors my inner geek far better than my husband.

When I call my sister in Colorado to tell her about my new discovery, she says, "You are becoming more like Dad every day." I smile, thinking about the tug of genetics. "Call me if you suddenly feel the urge to style you hair in a comb-over." And then almost as an afterthought, she adds, "You know, we have mountains out here, but we don't have lightning bugs. It's too dry."

"I know," I say. "It's a huge trade-off."

"Huge," she says. And there's a tiny silence between us, a silence full of twinkling memories.

★★★

Sabbath is a day for discovering (or rediscovering) the miraculous within the routine and the everyday. Pull up a lawn chair or find a soft seat by a window. Take time to relax and really enjoy your own backyard. Glance through a book about nature. Open an encyclopedia or your child's science book. Learn something new or remember something forgotten, something that will help you look at life in a new way and observe the familiar with awe. Let Sabbath leave you amazed.

## Sunday Dinner Menu

- Chicken and Rice Casserole
- Vegetable Salad with Dressing
- Sour Cream Dressing for Salad
- Blueberry Buckle
- Topping for Blueberry Buckle

# Chicken and Rice Casserole

## Ingredients

3 cups (675 g) of chicken, white meat, roasted
1 (13 1/2-ounce) (450 g) can of cream of mushroom soup
1 (13 1/2-ounce) (450 g) can cream of celery soup
1 (4 1/2-ounce) (153 g) can of mushrooms
1 cup (250 mL) of milk
8 ounces (240g) of quick cooking rice
8 ounces (240 g) of fried onion rings

## Preparation

In a large saucepan, add mushroom and celery soup. Gradually add milk, mixing until smooth. Add chicken, mushrooms, and rice. Cook on stove for 8–10 minutes, stirring often.

Pour mixture into a baking pan. Put onion rings on top. Bake 10–15 minutes at 350 degrees F (180 degrees C).

Serves 8. (Approximately 418 calories per serving.)

Adapted from Polly Hensley's "Chicken and Rice Casserole."

# Vegetable Salad with Dressing

## Ingredients

1 cup (225 g) of diced cucumbers
1 cup (225 g) of diced tomatoes
1 cup (225 g) of diced sweet onion
fresh salad greens of choice

## Preparation

Combine cucumbers, tomatoes, and onion. Toss lightly with sour cream dressing (see following). Arrange on a bed of crisp salad greens.

# Sour Cream Dressing for Vegetable Salad

## Ingredients

1 cup (225 g) of sour cream
1 tablespoon (15 mL) of vinegar
1 tablespoon (14 g) of horseradish sauce
1 teaspoon (4.6 g) of salt

## Preparation

Combine all ingredients in a small mixing bowl. Mix well.

Serves 6. (Approximately 110 calories per serving; includes dressing.)

Adapted from Mayme Pearson's "Vegetable Salad."

# Blueberry Buckle

## Ingredients

1/2 cup (120 g) of shortening
1/2 cup (120 g) of sugar
1 beaten egg
1 cup (225 g) of flour
1 1/2 teaspoons (6.9 g) of baking powder
1 teaspoon (4.6 g) of salt
1/3 cup (83 mL) of milk
2 cups (450 g) of blueberries

## Preparation

Cream the shortening and sugar. Add 1 beaten egg.

In a separate bowl, combine 1 1/2 teaspoons of baking powder, 1 teaspoon of salt, and 1 cup of sifted flour. Add powdered mixture to the first mixture, alternating with 1/3 cup of milk.

Pour into greased 8 × 8–inch pan. Scatter blueberries on top. Add topping.

# Topping for Blueberry Buckle

## Ingredients

1/2 cup (120 g) of sugar
1/2 cup (120 g) of flour
1/2 teaspoon (4.6 g) of cinnamon
1/2 cup (56 g) of butter

## Preparation

Mix sugar, flour, and cinnamon. Cut in butter. Sprinkle the topping mixture over berries. Bake 40 minutes at 350 degrees F (180 degrees C). Serve hot with ice cream.

Serves 6. (Approximately 603 calories per serving; includes one scoop of vanilla ice cream.)

Adapted from Mayme Pearson's, "North Shore Blueberry Buckle."

# Rethinking the Carving of Pumpkins

Sometimes I hold my life against the plumb line of my real life and my idealized life only to discover the two off kilter. Occasionally, I will daydream about finding the perfect job, having the perfect home, and of course, having the perfect body. The older I get, the more I can find humor in the width of the divide.

I seem to have created a fantasy family of imaginary people in my head. They are clones of my less-than-model family. They are perfect people who do perfect things at the perfect time, and I am their perfect matriarch.

Today at the grocery store while I was making a quick run for cat food and garbage bags, I purchased four large pumpkins. I spent a considerable amount of time choosing the best of the lot—large enough for a spooky faces, hollow enough for easy carving, nicely shaped, and flawlessly orange. I carried them one at a time into the house, setting them on the kitchen counter.

"Look!" I told my husband, pointing with enthusiasm at the faceless pumpkins. He simply nodded. No excitement. No real response. My fantasy husband would have reacted quite differently. He would have called the kids in to the kitchen and said, "Kids, come quick! It's time to carve the pumpkins!"

My fantasy children, being teenagers, would have hurried into the kitchen and said things like, "Way cool, Mom!" or, "Hey, I'm calling Dave. Four-wheeling will have to wait until my pumpkin is carved."

Instead my real son nodded (a characteristic he apparently learned from my husband) and said, "Mom, this is going to have to wait until I get back from Dave's house."

My real daughter smiled and said, "Can I take a nap first?"

My enthusiasm was dampened by my family's apathy. When did carving pumpkins become an eye-rolling, put-it-off-until-later chore? What would be next? Hanging stockings? Coloring Easter eggs? Making valentines?

I have never outgrown seasonal traditions, especially carving pumpkins. I have never grown tired of designing a unique edging for the top, of pulling seeds and pulp from the hollow center, of scraping the sides clean with a tablespoon, of cutting a distinctively ghoulish face, of lighting interior candles, and of dimming the lights for the full effect. In truth, I relish all of my family's seasonal traditions—all except one, namely my family's tradition of jumping in fall leaves.

My father was an amateur photographer who insisted on this yearly family tradition. He'd wait until an optimally sunny Sunday afternoon when lunch and naps were over, and he'd rally the troops, rakes in hand. We'd rake an impressive pile of crimson and gold while Dad set up his tripod and checked his light meter. Once the camera was in position, we'd jump into the leaves and toss them gleefully into the air as directed.

Colored leaves must be a photographer's catnip because my dad would become delirious with pleasure as he snapped the shutter again and again. I hated every minute of it every single year. My brother was far too rough, and my sister was far too whiny. I would usually get bashed in the mouth. The leaves would get hopelessly tangled in my hair, and I won't even discuss the year I endured the event in my brand-new training bra.

I did make an attempt at passing this tradition on to my children. Every magazine and every advertisement pictured autumn foliage and featured articles on fun-filled fall family activities. I began to feel the pressure to conform, certain that my fantasy family would revel in running through autumn leaves and that a perfect mother would not deny her children this experience. I raked a tremendous pile of oak and maple leaves beneath the shelter of their benefactors and called my children.

"Watch. I'll demonstrate," I said, backing up for takeoff. In perfect form I ran toward the leaves, pushed myself into an airborne half gainer, twisting onto my back, straightening the aerial stunt for a landing, and *thud*. My body dropped through the mound of leaves like a rock, slamming itself into a breathless stupor.

As I lie there, assessing my condition, attempting to determine if either of my lungs had collapsed, my seven-year-old son followed suit. Head back and chest extended, he executed a perfect airborne swan dive onto my face. I think my daughter said, "Mom, are you okay?" but she might have said, "Can I play?" Or maybe she said, "Ándale! Ándale! Ándale!" As I sat upright, she nailed me in the kidney with her green, glow-in-the-dark tennis shoes.

I crawled into the grass and watched as my children played in the leaves for about ninety additional seconds, grew bored, and went onto the house. I think my son said, "That was fun, Mom." But he might have said, "That was dumb, Mom." It's a blur. I was, after all, wounded.

After a while I noticed that my real husband and my real son, home from his friend's house, were focused on a football game. My real daughter was rested and talking to a friend on the phone, and four perfect pumpkins sat untouched and unnoticed on the kitchen counter. I began to feel uneasy.

Had my children simply tolerated the carving of pumpkins last year? Had their enjoyment been a game of pretense? Did they now abhor the slimy feel of wet pumpkin seeds and the artistic challenge of creating an original face? Was it all just a façade? Had I merely become a version my leaf-loving father?

"Mom!" my daughter said, startling me, "Are we going to carve our pumpkins?"

"Do you want to?" I asked her.

"What? Of course," she replied, looking the pumpkins over.

My son walked into kitchen. "I call first dibs on the pumpkins."

"I didn't think you were into it this year," I told him.

"Yeah right," my son said, grabbing a pumpkin.

Minutes later my husband poked his head into the kitchen. "Where's mine?" he asked. For an hour or so, the kitchen floor became a seasonal workshop, cluttered with garbage bags and wet globs of orange pulp.

As the sky turns dark, four jack-o'-lanterns glow in the darkness, three with unique faces and one with a giant hole for a face, my son's ambitious attempt to carve a peace sign. My real family is eating popcorn as a haunting melody heralds the cinematic tale of a teenage vampire slayer. I do not know what my fantasy family is doing right now, and I am simply too content to care.

★★★

Sabbath is a time for celebrating life. Real life. It is not a time to compare the life we have today with the perceived lives of others, with the fictionalized lives of television characters, with the romanticized versions of our past lives, or with the fantasy life that lives in the mind. The life we have today is full of precious moments we can't relive. There are no do-overs.

Today, take a stroll through your present-day life. Look at it with fresh eyes. Take note of the imperfections in your home. Look at your less-than-glamorous possessions. Take note of the people around you, people you love, people who don't live up to your expectations, people with their own set of strengths and weaknesses. Really look at them. Look at yourself. Look at your less-than-perfect self. Then thank your Creator for all of it.

Put your arms around your life, and accept it with love. Then celebrate!

153

## Sunday Dinner Menu

- Stuffed Zucchini Surprise
- Aunt Lettie's Icebox Rolls
- Apple Cider Salad
- Caramel Pie
- Meringue Topping for Caramel Pie

# Stuffed Zucchini Surprise

### Ingredients

3 small zucchini
1 cup (225 g) of sour cream
1 (8-ounce) (225 g) package of cream cheese
1/4 teaspoon (1.2 g) of garlic powder
1/4 teaspoon (1.2 g) of onion powder
1 cup (225 g) of sharp cheddar cheese

### Preparation

Clean whole zucchini and parboil for 5 minutes. Drain. Cut in half lengthwise. Spoon the zucchini from the shell. Save the shell. In a bowl, mix zucchini, cream cheese, garlic powder, onion powder, and cheese. Salt and pepper to taste. Fill shells and place in a baking pan. Bake at 350 degrees F (180 degrees C) for 30 minutes. Remove from oven, and spoon sour cream over individual shells. Return to oven, and bake for 10 more minutes.

Serves 6. (Approximately 306 calories per serving.)

Adapted from Polly Hensley's "Stuffed Zucchini Surprise."

# Aunt Lettie's Icebox Rolls

## Ingredients

3/4 cup (169 g) of shortening
3/4 cup (169 g) of sugar
1 teaspoon (4.6 g) of salt
1 cup (250 mL) of boiling water
2 cakes or packages of yeast
1 cup (250 mL) of lukewarm water
2 eggs, beaten
4 tablespoons (60 g) of melted butter
6 cups of flour (plus a little more for kneading)

## Preparation

In a bowl, blend salt and shortening. Add one cup of boiling water, and mix. Set aside to cool.

In a separate bowl, dissolve yeast cakes or packages in one cup of lukewarm water. Stir gently until the yeast is dissolved.

When salt and shortening is lukewarm, add dissolved yeast. Add beaten eggs and mix. Add flour.

Place dough into a greased bowl, and cover bowl with a dish towel. Allow dough to rise in a warm place free from drafts until light and double in size (2–3 hours).

Punch and roll out about 1/2 inch thick. Using a biscuit cutter, cut rolls. Brush with butter, and fold in half. Place on baking pans and cover with a dish towel.

Allow rolls to rise in a warm place free from drafts for about 3 hours. Bake at 425 degrees F (230 degrees C) until brown.

Makes 18–20 rolls. (Approximately 267 calories per roll.)

Adapted from my Great-Aunt Lettie's "Icebox Rolls."

# Apple Cider Salad

## Ingredients

2 (3 1/2-ounce) (105 g) boxes of apple or lemon-flavored gelatin
2 cups (500 mL) hot water
2 cups (450 mL) of apple cider
2 cups (450 mL) diced, unpeeled apples
3/4 cups (169 g) nuts, coarsely broken
1 (16-ounce) (480 g) container of sour cream

## Preparation

Empty the gelatin into a bowl. Add hot water, and stir until gelatin is dissolved. Add cider. Chill until slightly thick. Fold in apples and nuts. Pour into mold or 8 × 8–inch pan.

Refrigerate until set.

Serves 8. (Approximately 380 calories per serving.)

Adapted from Mayme Pearson's "Apple Cider Salad."

# Caramel Pie

## Ingredients

1 cup (225 g) of brown sugar
1/2 cup (125 g) of sugar
1/4 teaspoon (1.2 g) of salt
4 tablespoons (120 g) of flour
4 tablespoons (120 g) of real butter
4 egg yolks (reserve whites for meringue)
2 cups (500 mL) of cream
1 teaspoon (5 mL) of vanilla
baked premade pie crust

## Preparation

Mix dry ingredients. Beat egg yolks and cream. Slowly add wet mixture to dry mixture. Add butter, and cook in double boiler until thick. Add vanilla and blend. Pour into baked pie shell. Top with meringue.

# Meringue Topping for Caramel Pie

## Ingredients

3 egg whites
6 tablespoons (180 g) of sugar
1/2 teaspoon (2.4 mL) of vanilla

## Preparation

Beat egg whites until frothy. Gradually add sugar, continuing to beat the eggs until they form stiff peaks. Add vanilla and mix into egg whites. Spread on pie. Make sure to spread meringue to the edges of the crust to seal.

Bake at 325 degrees F (160 degrees C) for 15–16 minutes until nicely browned.

Serves 8. (Approximately 289 calories per piece; includes meringue.)

Adapted from Polly Hensley's "Caramel Pie."

# The Gift of Ironing and Other Tedious Chores

I have a basket of ironing that is three and a half feet tall. It is a monument to procrastination and busyness. Actually our entire home has become a monument to procrastination and busyness. Today a choice had to be made. I had to clean the house or have a nervous breakdown. Either pick up two weeks' worth of clutter or go to a soft, padded room and sleep? Either spray furniture wax or take sedatives? It was a tough decision.

After only a few hours of dedication to home and hearth, the kitchen smells like a pine forest. The floor has been adequately scraped, and I was finally able to locate the toaster. A thousand scrubbing bubbles and one tough gal with a sponge have scoured the bathrooms.

Having spent a mere forty minutes selecting appropriate music for the task, my husband is preparing to vacuum. Vacuuming is the job I delegate if at all possible. I despise running the vacuum, and it's the one part of housework that can be done with a real machine—Mach 3.8, fifteen amps of pure power, and a six-stage air filtration system; my husband likes machines.

The kids are cleaning their rooms, under duress, of course. I think their exact words were, "Mom, you're not supposed to work on Sunday."

I think my exact words were, "If you ever want to see your friends again, get to cleaning." This job will take my daughter three and half hours. My son will finish in fifteen minutes flat.

Now I know the Creator made all and declared it good, and for that, we set aside a day of the week to rest and be grateful. But let's also keep in mind that this same Creator made dust mites, bedbugs, cats that puke hairballs, and dirty underwear. Yes, God made dirty underwear, the 100 percent cotton fiber, the butt that dirtied them, and the brain that left them in the middle of the bathroom floor. While I am well aware of the rule about not working on the Sabbath, I am also aware that there are petrified cornflakes on the kitchen floor, dried peanut butter on the refrigerator door, and curdled milk in at least fourteen drinking glasses. My mind will not allow me to rest until the house is clean.

As Bruce Springsteen sings about his glory days and as my husband fires up his fifteen amps of pure power, I seek the partial solitude of the downstairs den, where I begin to iron, a job I find relaxing. I have honestly loved to iron since the first time my mother lowered the ironing board to the six-year-old position, turned the iron on low, and let me iron a pile of my baby brother's diapers and a few bath towels. I do not admit this to my family. If I did, I would lose a major manipulative tool. I could not say things like, "Why are you complaining about taking one little bag of trash to the garage? Have you seen the basket of ironing downstairs? That's what I get to do tonight." And there's never a defense because there is always a basket of ironing.

I am watching a TV news program, the kind with short, interesting stories that I can mostly listen to as I smooth wrinkles from the twenty-seven T-shirts my son did not fold directly from the dryer. There is something satisfying about ironing my husband's simple cotton work shirts while listening to stories about the outrageous antics of the wealthy, the renowned, and the celebrated. There is something comforting about flattening unruly collars and creased cuffs while stories of human disaster and human humiliation waft intensified and inflated above a dramatic soundtrack. There is something agreeable about pressing denim jeans, especially those faded to an unpretentious pale blue, while politicians squirm and evade. TV tends to exaggerate and frighten. Ironing seems to smooth and restore. I am grateful for the contradiction.

I also like the smell of spray starch and the warmth of the ironing board. I like the look of the clothes hanging crisply on hangers and lying in neatly folded little piles. I like the empty laundry basket, however temporary. Some people search out the exotic and the faraway to feel contented. Some find contentment by restoring order and cleanliness to the place they call home. Some seek high, holy places and attend spiritual retreats in order to meditate deeply on life, and some merely iron on a Sunday afternoon.

★★★

True rest and relaxation are difficult in an environment of chaos and disarray. The restoration of order and cleanliness to our homes can revive and rejuvenate contentment. Clearing clutter can create a sense of calm. Dusting and sweeping can ease anxiety. Folding clothes or making the beds can renew an appreciation for what is simple and uncomplicated. Tending to our homes on the Sabbath need not be considered work if the tasks are done with sincere appreciation for the gifts given and they are followed by a long luxurious nap on fresh sheets.

*Paula Hartman*

## Sunday Dinner Menu

- Five O'clock Casserole
- Glorified Green Beans
- Peaches Paree

---

## Five O'clock Casserole

---

### Ingredients

1 1/2 pounds (675 g) of round steak
1 cup (225 g) of flour
1/4 cup (60 mL) of vegetable oil
2 (13 1/2-ounce) (495 g) cans of diced tomatoes
1 medium onion, thinly sliced
1/4 cup (56 g) diced green pepper
1/4 cup (56 g) of instant rice
1/2 cup (125 mL) of water
1 1/2 teaspoons (6.9 g) of salt
1/8 teaspoon (0.5 g) of pepper

### Preparation

Cut round steak into small pieces. Dredge with flour. Place vegetable oil in a skillet. When the oil is very hot, brown the round steak on all sides.

Place the meat in a casserole dish that's 1 1/2 quarts in size. Add tomatoes, onion, pepper, rice, water, salt, and pepper. Cover and bake at 350 degrees F (180 degrees C) for 1 1/2 hours.

Serves 6. (Approximately 451 calories per serving.)

Adapted from Mayme Pearson's "Five O'clock Casserole."

# Glorified Green Beans

## Ingredients

1 (16-ounce) (480 g) can of green beans (preferably whole)
3 tablespoons (45 mL) of olive oil
3/4 cup (169 g) thinly sliced or chopped onion
1 tablespoon (14 g) of prepared mustard
1 tablespoon (14 g) of horseradish sauce
Salt and pepper to taste

## Preparation

In a saucepan, cook onion in olive oil until soft and golden. (If you want to use fresh green beans, cook the beans until tender before cooking the onion). Drain green beans. Add to onion. Add mustard and horseradish sauce. Add salt and pepper to taste. Simmer until hot.

Serves 6. (Approximately 119 calories per serving.)

Adapted from Mayme Pearson's "Glorified Green Beans."

## Peaches Paree

### Ingredients

2 (15-ounce) (450 g) cans of cling peach slices in unsweetened juice
1 1/2 teaspoons (45 mL) of lemon juice
1/8 teaspoon (0.5 g) of cinnamon
1/2 teaspoon (2 mL) of vanilla

### Preparation

Pour peaches with juice into a saucepan. Before turning on the heat, add lemon juice, cinnamon, and vanilla. Cook on low for about 15 minutes to allow flavors to blend.

Drain peaches. Serve with a slice of angel food cake or pound cake.

Serves 6. (Approximately 129 calories per serving; includes one slice of angel food cake.)

Adapted from Mayme Pearson's recipe "Peaches Paree."

# SUNDAY #23

# A Gathering of Wise Women

I am a little tired, having worked a long, tedious Sunday. It's been the kind of day that wears you out just by the slowness of its passing. A nap would be nice, but I have preparations to make before my friend Filly arrives. I have jars to wash and sterilize, lids and rings to boil, and coffee to make. Filly and I are making cherry jam.

The summers as I was growing up always included the canning of vegetables, the processing of pickles, and the making of jellies and jams. It was an ongoing family project that filled long afternoons and nearly every Saturday in August. We picked and shelled peas. We snapped beans by the bushel. We stood over garbage cans in the backyard, shucked baskets of sweet corn, fighting off the bees that swarmed the husks and tossing corn silks at one another. We scraped corn, sliced beets, chopped peppers, and minced onions.

Only my sister and I helped with the actual canning. It was an exact science that our mother explained in careful detail. "You have to do it right," she would say, "or you'll give your family food poisoning." We sterilized the jars and lids in pans of boiling water. We cooked and seasoned the vegetables in large kettles, ladling them into hot jars. Air bubbles were removed with a table knife, and the rims of the jars were wiped completely clean. "Even a grain of salt on the rim of the jar will keep it from sealing." Mom would tell us. The sterilized lids were put into place and secured finger-tight with gold canning rings.

Some vegetables were processed in the cold packer and boiled on the stove until sterile. Other vegetables went into the pressure cooker, a heavy steel pan that hissed and whistled. Mom would clear the kitchen before she took the lid off the pressure cooker. She'd warn us, "These things have been known to explode." We'd peak through the doorway, watching tensely as mom carefully turned the lid to release the last gasp of stream from the ominous silver pan. It was like watching a munitions expert diffuse a bomb.

In early August, we'd travel to Kentucky, where our mother and her mother would make pickles, dill and sweet. To this day, a sprig of dill transports me to that kitchen, where cucumber slices soaked in kettles of salty brine while Mom and Granny smoked and gossiped, the air perfumed by spice, vinegar, onion, tobacco smoke, and dill.

We'd make jellies and jams as the fruit came into season. May was the month for strawberry freezer jam. In late June, we'd make spiced blueberry jam and sometimes raspberry or blackberry preserves. July was the season of honeyed peach conserve. Sour cherries arrived in August. September was the time for making Concord grape and cinnamon apple jellies. When we were done, we'd sit outside, watch the lightning bugs, and listen through the screen door for the pings of jelly jars sealing.

Filly arrives with twenty pounds of pitted sour cherries and enough prepared dough for two cherry pies. The cherries are beautiful, the deep red of December velvet. We each try a cherry, chewing with squinted faces, laughing like two little girls sucking on sour jawbreakers. A warm, humid breeze carries the scent of mowed grass and pinesap through the open kitchen window. The steaming kettle on the stove intensifies the heat as we maneuver the kitchen in bare feet, the conversation rolling faster than the water in the canner.

Four hours and a whole pot of coffee later, we have forty jars of jam cooling on the kitchen counter and two cherry pies baking in the oven. We are sticky. Our hair clings to our necks in damps strands as we sit on the porch swing to cool down. We swing back and forth in silence, basking in the familiarity of each other.

"We are just like sisters," Filly says. This is the sweetest blessing a woman can bestow upon another. Even while wearing smudged mascara, standing in bare feet and with shorts spotted with cherry juice, I am accepted. The wind chime in the corner rings like the bells from a faraway steeple, and friendship dances like fairy light, swirling in the tender night air as jelly jars begin to ping one by one.

★★★

Wise women gather to cook, sew, and create. Wise women cherish the modest work that allows children to play nearby, encourages one to work in bare feet, makes good use of the wisdom that comes with age and is best done while chatting. Wise women understand that the work done at the kitchen table can sustain a family, deepen a friendship, and cement a community. They understand that with the passing of time, a gathering of women can become a thread of ritual that will connect one soul to another like a rosary.

Today, invite a friend into your home to chat and create. Prepare a special meal. Make candy. Bake bread. Quilt. Paint. As you share in the joy of this sacred work, remember that where wise women gather, where the kettle is put to boiling and the dough is readied for rolling, here the spirit of Sabbath makes herself at home. She kicks off her shoes, pours herself a cup of coffee, and joins those gathered in her holy kitchen.

## Sunday Dinner Menu

- Macaroni and Cheese
- Wilted Spinach Salad
- Corn-Stuffed Tomatoes
- Frozen Ice Cream Ring

# Macaroni and Cheese

## Ingredients

4 tablespoons (56 g) of margarine
2 tablespoons (28 g) of flour
1 1/2 (375 mL) cups of milk
1 teaspoon (4.6 g) of salt
1/8 (0.5 g) teaspoon of pepper
1 cup (225 g) of grated cheddar cheese
8 ounces (225 g) of uncooked macaroni
Seasoned breadcrumbs

## Preparation

Melt butter in a saucepan. Add flour, salt, and pepper. Cook for 1 minute. Gradually add the milk and mix. Add cheese and mix until thick and smooth.

Cook macaroni. Spoon half of the macaroni into a buttered 2-quart baking dish. Add half of the sauce. Repeat. Sprinkle with seasoned breadcrumbs. Bake at 350 degrees F (180 degrees C) until mixture bubbles and the breadcrumbs are lightly browned.

Serves 6. (Approximately 392 calories per serving.)

Adapted from Mayme Pearson's "Macaroni and Cheese."

# Wilted Spinach Salad

## Ingredients

2 slices (28 g) of bacon, fried and chopped, save drippings
1/2 cup (125 mL) of vinegar
1 beaten egg
1/2 cup (125 mL) of water
1 tablespoon (14 g) of sugar
1/2 teaspoon (2.3 g) of salt
1 minced onion
6 ounces (180 g) of spinach or leaf lettuce

## Preparation

Tear lettuce or spinach into bite-size pieces. Place in a serving dish. Mix bacon with drippings, vinegar, beaten egg, water, sugar, salt, and onion in a saucepan. Heat until very hot. While mixture is hot, pour over lettuce.

Serves 6. (Approximately 86 calories per serving.)

Adapted from Polly Hensley's "Wilted Lettuce Salad."

# Corn-Stuffed Tomatoes

## Ingredients

6 large, firm tomatoes
1 1/2 cups (345 g) of corn kernels
1/2 cup (120 g) chopped green onions
1/2 cup (120 g) of chopped green pepper
1 teaspoon (4.6 g) of salt
4 tablespoons (125 mL) of olive oil
1 teaspoon (5 mL) of lemon juice or vinegar
1 large clove of garlic, minced

## Preparation

Cut out tomato cores. Cut each into wedges but not quite through. Spoon most of the centers of the tomatoes. Invert tomato cups. Drain and chill.

In a bowl, chop tomato pulp finely, and then drain. Mix drained corn, tomatoes, onions, green pepper, and salt. Set aside.

In a small bowl, whisk together olive oil, lemon juice, garlic, salt, and pepper. Pour over vegetables, and mix well. Chill.

At serving time, spoon mix into chilled tomato cups. Serve.

Serves 6. (Approximately 138 calories per serving.)

Adapted from Polly Hensley's "Corn-Stuffed Tomatoes."

# Frozen Ice Cream Ring

## Ingredients

1 pint (450 g) of orange sherbet
1 pint (450 g) of raspberry sherbet
1 quart (900 g) of vanilla ice cream
1 cored pineapple, cut into very small pieces
1 pint (450 g) of fresh strawberries, sliced
1 pint (450 g) of frozen whipped cream, thawed

Just a note: This recipe will work with many combinations of sherbet and ice cream, so experiment and enjoy.

## Preparation

Shape the sherbet and into small scoops or balls. Place on a cookie sheet, and place in freezer. Soften vanilla ice cream. Fold in fresh pineapple. Pour half of the mixture into the bottom of an angel food cake pan or Bundt cake pan. Arrange sherbet balls on top. Pour remaining ice cream mixture around and over the balls. Place in freezer until ice cream is firm.

Remove the ice cream ring from the pan, placing it on a plate or serving tray. Frost with whipped cream. Garnish with fresh strawberries.

Serves 12. (Approximately 226 calories per serving.)

Adapted from Polly Hensley's recipe, "Frozen Ice Cream Ring"

## SUNDAY #24

# A Walk in a Wooded Memory

There is a county park near our home called Hubbard Valley, which was named, I suppose, for the Hubbards, who were perhaps a family with a wagon, a dog, and the need to settle down. A sign beside the map of walking trails and a list of park rules states that the park was once the home of an Indian village. I wonder what happened to the Indians? Were they forced by treaty to a lesser place, or did they just move on? I tell myself that I should learn the history of this place, this small town in Ohio where I have lived now for ten years. But that is for another day. Today the ground, the trees, and the clear sky will hold the silent knowledge of what went before as I walk with my husband in the present of this Sunday morning.

We take to the walking trail, clad in shorts, sneakers, and ample bug spray. Our dog, Molly, strains on her leash, eager to follow a trail of new and unique odors. The trail is a little muddy and a little slick. It's been a wet summer, very wet. The foliage is buzzing with insect sounds and birdsongs.

We walk briskly. Molly allows no Disneyland strolling. Sometimes I wonder who is walking whom. My husband laughs as she pulls me down a small dip on the path, my feet moving as wildly as a child on ice skates. I am relieved to find myself standing upright at the bottom, where a patch of wildflowers and tall weeds strain for the mottled sunlight falling between two oak trees. The ground is a mosaic of fallen branches, moss-covered logs, wild ivy, ferns, and the mulch of summers past. A steady, warm breeze creates a moving canopy that whispers above our heads and above the chaotic beauty of the wooded floor.

As we emerge from the woods, the path circles around the edge of Hubbard Valley Lake, where a man and a young boy are fishing. Cattails stand like sentinels in the shallow water near the lake shore as a group of wild geese wander about the dock, honking. The lake banks are covered in pink wildflowers whose name I do not know, but their fragrance reminds me of the honeysuckles that once climbed the trellis beside my grandparent's front stoop.

I think back to my grandparents' hundred-acre farm in Kentucky, much of which was a rocky, rolling foothill of the Appalachian Mountains. I remember walking there with my father and my grandfather—my grandfather with his silver hair and square jaw, a weaver dressed in overalls and a plaid work shirt, walking beside his dog, Jock, my gentle grandfather striding through the woods like a mountain man.

I recall my father bending to pick a sprig of mountain teaberry, telling me to bite it with my teeth. Its mint is forever etched into my memory. We would usually walk to a field of wild daffodils, an oasis of glorious yellow in the middle of the woods. The field was the ancient site of an Indian tribe. When visiting my grandparents, we would often walk there to search for arrowheads and artifacts. My sister and I would pick bouquets of flowers for my mother and my grandmother, who always stayed at the house, contently drinking iced tea, smoking, and talking at my grandparents' kitchen table.

I remember my grandmother's hazel eyes and her dark skin, so like my father's. I remember her hair, which was as black as Kentucky coal, and the fierceness in her face, even when she smiled. I remember that she saved coupons from the back of her cigarette packs and let us choose gifts from the redemption catalog. I remember that in an age when good women were required to be good mothers and good housekeepers, she was neither.

Our dog, Molly, jerks me back to the present, lurching forward on her leash, pulling me toward a woman with a German shepherd coming in the opposite direction. I quickly hand the leash to my husband. He pulls it tightly as the two canines sniff each other in some ancient greeting, long forgotten by those of us who are civilized. I watch Molly simply being who she was born to be, quivering with the excitement of meeting another creature like her. And I think about my wild grandmother holding her bouquet of mountain-grown daffodils, and a small yellow butterfly, its flight filled with reckless vitality, sweeps across our path.

★★★

Sabbath time is a time for walking, a time for planting your feet rhythmically upon the earth, for moving without a destination, whether in a nearby woods or along the sidewalk in your neighborhood. It's not a time for treadmills or power walking. Walking in Sabbath time is gentle and slow. It does not decrease your waistline. It allows you to stretch and to quiet your mind. Sabbath provides a quiet space where the past can come calling and fold itself tenderly into the present. It has the power to heal.

Today, put on your walking shoes and take off for a walk. Walk until you are feeling calm and relaxed. Allow your senses to absorb what you see and hear and smell. Let your mind drift from image to image, from memory to memory softly and without judgment until you are in a lovely new place called today.

## Sunday Dinner Menu

- Pot Roast with Gravy
- Gravy for Pot Roast
- Buttered Noodles
- Pineapple and Cherry Salad

## Pot Roast with Gravy

### Ingredients

1 (4-pound) (1.92 kg) beef roast (rib, sirloin, or rump)
1 clove of garlic
2 teaspoons (9.2 g) of salt
3 tablespoons (42 g) of flour
1 tablespoon (30 mL) of vegetable oil
6 medium potatoes, peeled and sliced in half
12 pared carrots
8 medium onions, skins removed and sliced in half

### Preparation

Rub roast with cut surface of garlic. Discard garlic. Sprinkle with salt. Allow roast to sit for 10–15 minutes.

Rub roast with flour. On stovetop in a large heavy skillet, heat oil. When hot, add roast, and brown the roast on all sides. Takes about 15–20 minutes for good browning.

Place the roast in a Dutch oven or large roasting pan. If possible, slip a low rack under the meat to keep it out of liquid. This also prevents burning during cooking. Do not add water.

Cook roast for 50–60 minutes per pound at 350 degrees F (180 degrees C). Add vegetables an hour before serving. Cook until meat and vegetables are tender. Remove roast and vegetables from pan and keep warm. Reserve drippings for gravy. Makes 10–12 servings.

# Gravy for Pot Roast

## Ingredients

Pot roast drippings and water (or other fluid) to equal 3 cups (750 mL) of liquid
6 tablespoons (84 g) of flour
Salt and pepper

## Preparation

Remove roast from pan. Use measuring cup to measure the amount of drippings remaining.

Place the drippings into a saucepan. Without heating, gradually add 6 tablespoons of flour, stirring until the flour is well blended with drippings. Add enough water (milk, beef stock, or tomato juice can be substituted for water, if desired) to equal 3 cups of liquid. Cook and stir until gravy thickens. Salt and pepper to taste.

Serves 12. (Approximately 25 calories per 1/4 cup serving.)

Adapted from Mayme Pearson's, "Covered Pot Roast."

## Buttered Noodles

### Ingredient

16 ounces (450 g) of packaged egg noodles
2 teaspoons (9.2 g) of salt
1/4 cup (56 g) of melted margarine

### Preparation

Bring 3–4 quarts of water to a boil. Add salt. (This will season your noodles while they are cooking.) Cook noodles according to package directions until tender. Drain water and place in a serving bowl. Cover with melted butter or margarine, and mix well.

Serves 12. (Approximately 85 calories per 1/4 cup (56g) serving.)

From the kitchen of Paula Hartman.

## Pineapple and Cherry Salad

### Ingredients

1 (14 1/2-ounce) (435 g) can of crushed pineapple
1 (14 1/2-ounce) (435 g) can of cherry pie filling
1 (10-ounce) (300 mL) can of sweetened, condensed milk
1 (16-ounce) (480 g) container of frozen whipped cream, thawed

### Preparation

In a large mixing bowl, mix all ingredients together. Place in a long baking dish, and freeze. Take out of freezer 10 minutes before serving.

Serves 12. (Approximately 170 calories per serving.)

Adapted from Polly Hensley's "Pink Salad."

# SUNDAY #25

---

# The Curse of Heredity

I stand in awe of anyone who possesses an innate sense of direction, the genetic gift that enables them to successfully maneuver a maze of tangled expressways or to navigate a city labyrinth of one-way streets, all the while saying things like, "Now I know we want to go east," or, "I think East Main runs north and south." I say this because giving me a set of directions that reads, "Go north on First Street, and then turn west on Broad," and expecting me to arrive at my destination is analogous to giving my dog a recipe for chocolate chip cookies and expecting actual cookies. I need someone to simply say, "Turn left. Turn right." I need landmarks, and I need a person to tell me, "If you come to a set of railroad tracks beside the Hob-Knob Diner, you've gone too far." I need little maps with arrows and little labeled buildings and emergency phone numbers.

I am the daughter of a man who once circled Chicago for two hours because he could not find his way off the bypass. This same man said to my mother, "We're lost." This same man snarled at his wife, "You're the one with the map!" This same man watched as his wife rolled down her window and let the map fly away like some strange winged creature of the night.

My seven-year-old self did not know I was witnessing the age-old battle between a man who will not ask directions and a woman having difficulty reading the map. I did not know that saying, "We're lost," meant only that we were temporarily lost. I thought it meant that we were lost forever, that we were never getting out of Illinois, "Hansel

178

and Gretel" lost. I did not know that upon stopping for directions, my dad could also get another map.

I am the daughter of a woman who was profoundly night blind. This same woman missed driveways, drove into yards, drove into fields, drove over curbs, and missed freeway exits, all the while asking, "What did that sign say?"

I did not understand that a small road sign was meaningless unless you could read it. I did not understand that landmarks were useless if you could not see them. I didn't understand how much a driveway and patch of grass could resemble each other. And I did not know that night blindness was a genetically inherited trait that made it necessary on occasion to enter a convenient store and ask a teenage boy in a do-rag and with a pierced face, "Can you tell me what town I am in?"

Tonight my friend Renee and I took twelve teenage girls from our church to a Christmas concert in Cleveland. Normally, I would have refused to drive because I am night blind, but Renee could not fit all fourteen of us into her minivan. She assured me that she would drive slowly and not loose me in the city. (I know how Renee drives. She drives at only one speed, way too fast.)

The trip up was uneventful, and the concert was great. It was only as we turned out of the parking garage to go home that the night took a perilous turn toward the shadowy streets of the lost. I'm not even sure how it happened. There was the initial rush of five hundred automobiles racing toward one small exit from the parking garage. There was a woman in a silver car that prevented me from following directly behind Renee, thrusting her car in front of mine, daring me to crush her left door with my bumper. There was a man in a fluorescent orange coat waving a flag with great authority. There was a glorious Christmas tree stretching in white light up the side of the building, which ever-so-briefly caught my attention. There were four teenage girls in the car, all talking simultaneously. I looked up, and *poof*, Renee was gone.

Trying to remain calm, I told the girls, "I've lost Renee, and now we all have to look out for the expressway." I then proceeded to turn left and right and left again and right again, taking the girls for an impromptu tour of Cleveland. We drove into a neighborhood where old houses were rundown and characters in hooded sweatshirts walked about like creatures from *The Night of the Living Dead*. I ordered the girls to get their beautiful, sweet faces away from the windows, to sit back, and to attempt to look ugly.

I know the young man who stepped toward the curb was probably just planning to cross the street, but there had been a recent carjacking in the news. Sitting at a stop sign, I imagined being pulled from car at gunpoint. I imagined watching my car pull away with beautiful, sweet faces looking desperately out the back window. The innocent kid, who was probably just walking to his girlfriend's house, suddenly looked about seven feet tall with mangled teeth, liquored-up breath, and psychotic eyes. So I panicked. I hit the gas and made a quick right-hand turn onto a one-way street, so I was going the wrong way.

The girls began commenting on our situation. "I think you might be going the wrong way."

"I think that sign said, 'No right turn!'"

"I don't think those headlights are supposed to be coming toward us."

I hit the brakes and screeched to the curb. I trembled in silence as two cars passed, scolding me with their horns, their drivers mouthing what I did not think were reassuring comments. Resting my forehead against the steering wheel, I began to mutter in a language usually attributed to drunken sailors.

"Did you say something?" Sarah asked from the backseat.

My copilot, Kelly, a young woman who was mature and wise beyond her years, said, "She is just praying out loud."

We eventually found the expressway, thanks to a nice older couple we met at a red light that had pity on us and allowed us to follow them out of Cleveland. I took the girls to their respective homes, missing Kelly's driveway twice. (This is what usually happens every single time I take Kelly home at night.). Having safely returned the girls to their families, to whom they will undoubtedly tell the tale of "Lost in Cleveland with Paula," I turn my car toward the one place where there are no confusing signs, where roads do not lurch and detour, where exits ramps do not hurl me into unknown dark places. I head toward my one true north—home.

★★★

Sabbath is a day for returning home, a day for returning to the place where we are known and cherished. It is a day for realigning ourselves with what gives our lives their truest sense of direction. Explore a new place today. Take an unfamiliar road. Survey novel scenery. But in the traveling, turn your soul's compass toward the divine, and keep your sight ever pointed toward home.

## Sunday Dinner Menu

- Chicken Salad
- Vegetable Soup for Crock-Pot
- Chocolate Chip Cookies

## Chicken Salad

### Ingredients

6 cups (1.35 kg) of chicken, white meat, roasted
5 tablespoons (150 g) of French dressing
2 cups (450 g) of chopped celery
3 teaspoons (14 g) of grated onion
2 dill pickles, chopped
2 hard-boiled eggs, chopped
4 tablespoons (56 g) of mayonnaise
1/2 teaspoon (2.3 g) of salt
1/4 teaspoon (0.5 g) of pepper
2 teaspoons (9.2 g) of paprika
Washed lettuce leaves for serving
Additional paprika for garnish

### Preparation

Place chicken in a mixing bowl. Drizzle with French dressing, and toss. Chill for one hour.

Add celery, pickles, onion, and chopped eggs. Mix. Add mayonnaise, salt, and pepper. Mix well. Serve on lettuce. Garnish with a sprinkle of paprika, if desired.

Adapted from Mayme Pearson's "Chicken Salad."

# Vegetable Soup for Crock-Pot

## Ingredients

1 (4-ounce) (120 g) can of corn
1 (4-ounce) (120 g) can of green beans
1 (4-ounce) (120 g) can of chopped potatoes
1 (4-ounce) (120 g) can of carrots
2 tablespoons (30 mL) of olive oil
1 medium onion, chopped
1 cup (225 g) of chopped celery
1 (32-ounce) (960 mL) can or box of vegetable broth
2 teaspoons (9.6 g) of paprika
1/2 teaspoon (2.3 g) of celery seed
1 teaspoon (4.6 g) of sea salt
1 (32-ounce) (960 mL) can of tomato juice
8 ounces (225 g) of uncooked macaroni

## Preparation

In a small skillet or sauté pan, heat olive oil. Add chopped onion and celery. Cook until the onion is translucent. Add onion and celery along with oil to Crock-Pot.

Add corn, green beans, potatoes, and carrots. Cover with broth. Add paprika, celery seed, and salt. Finish filling Crock-Pot with tomato juice. (Cook on low for 8–10 hours.)

Stir occasionally, and add additional tomato juice as the broth cooks down.

About half an hour before serving, cook macaroni according to manufacturer's directions. Add to soup. Adding the macaroni when soup is made will make it mushy.

Before serving, add additional salt and pepper to taste.

Serves 8. (Approximately 75 calories per serving)

From the kitchen of Paula Hartman.

# Chocolate Chip Cookies

## Ingredients

1 cup (225 g) of margarine
1 cup (225 g) of shortening
1 1/2 cups (345 g) of brown sugar
1 1/2 cups (345 g) of white sugar
4 eggs
2 teaspoons (10 mL) of vanilla
1 teaspoon (4.6 g) of salt
2 teaspoons (9.2 g) of baking soda
5 cups (1.12 kg) of flour
1 (12-ounce) (360 g) bag of chocolate chips

## Preparation

Preheat oven to 375 degrees F (190 degrees C). In a large mixing bowl, using an electric mixer, cream butter or margarine, shortening, brown sugar, and white sugar. Add eggs and vanilla, and mix well.

Add salt, baking soda, and flour, and mix well. Fold in chocolate chips. Scoop out cookies and place on an ungreased cookie sheet. Bake 8–9 minutes.

Makes approximately 5-dozen cookies.

Serving size: one cookie. (Approximately 162 calories per serving.)

Adapted from the Schlembach's "Chocolate Chip Cookies."

# Dearest Diary

It is one of those Sunday afternoons when my household has temporarily grown larger. Everyone has company. My son and his girlfriend, Jenna, are gathering supplies for an afternoon of fishing at the large pond on my mother-in-law's property. We have been trying to restock our own pond, which we drained and repacked with clay last summer. The fishing will involve the capture of live bass, their transport in buckets via my son's red pickup truck, and their release from captivity.

I ask my son if he will sing "Born Free" as he sets the fish free, and he looks at me blankly. He does not know what I am talking about, and I feel momentarily older. "You know, 'Born free … as free as the wind blows,'" I sing. "It's a song from a movie." Jenna flashes one of those sympathetic smiles you give very, very old women wearing pink crocheted sweaters that smell of mothballs.

My daughter and her boyfriend leave to take our dog to the park for a long walk and an ice cream cone, but only after I spray each of them liberally with bug spray, explaining that the bugs by the lake are vicious. "Vicious," I tell them and show them the bites I received on my walk the day before. Emily smiles at her boyfriend, who smiles back, and once again, I feel like an old woman, only this time I am showing a perfect stranger the scar from my triple bypass.

My husband's best friend is visiting from Minneapolis. They are engrossed in a baseball game, their feet propped on the coffee table, the room heady with testosterone and resurrected high school camaraderie.

It is the top of the second inning. I ask about the score, but only to be polite. I do not enjoy baseball unless one of my own children is playing, and even then I tend to lose track of the game. So I leave the men to their game. I will rejoin my family later when the fish are free, the dog is tired and sleeping beside the sofa, and the extra innings area things of the past. We will put hamburgers on the grill for supper, and there will be talk of bass, baseball, and vicious bugs that draw blood.

For now I have a rare moment of solitude. I grab my notebook and pen, walk to the back porch, and begin to journal.

> Today I am recuperating from Emily's graduation party. Special events make me miss Mom and Dad so much that I sort of overcompensate on everything. I invited nearly sixty people. Yes, sixty. I guess I just wanted the house to be full of people who love Emily. And to be honest, I didn't think everyone would come, but almost everyone did. The RSVPs just keep coming.
>
> I have barely slept this week, worrying that there would not be enough food to feed everyone. I was afraid that we would run out of food, and out of desperation, I would start serving cornflakes and canned soup. So I ordered more food and went back to the grocery store for more supplies.
>
> I have cleaned like a possessed woman, fearing, I guess, that one of our guests might open a cabinet in the bathroom and discover the disarray I hide from others. If Janell had not come up on Saturday to help me cook, I would probably have had to pull an all-nighter. As it was, we were up until two in the morning. On Sunday, we went to church, exhausted from cooking and cleaning. I knelt after Communion and actually prayed, "Lord, if you fed five thousand people with two fishes and five loaves of bread, with leftovers, please help

me feed sixty people with three circle subs and a large pan of roasted chicken."

The ceremony, held on the football field, began beautifully. Emily was one of the first to graduate. (She looked very happy.) Then a strange thing happened. With 312 graduates to go, the sun disappeared behind a dense blanket of clouds. The temperature dropped by at least ten degrees, and the wind began to whip through the bleachers. Janell had worn only a tiny little dress. I mean, it was tiny. We were all cold, but she was freezing. She told me, "Mom, I think they need to speed things up a bit. They should stop using the full names and just read like the first initial and make them run. G, go. M, go. W, go. Go! Faster, faster!"

Emily's party turned out nicely. Everyone ate and ate, and we still had enough leftovers to last the rest of the week. The best part of graduation day happened when I stuck my head in the door of Emily's room to tell her good night. She was sitting on her bed, surrounded by her graduation cards and crumbled wrapping paper. "Mom, thanks so much for the party. I just can't believe that all these people love me, really love me."

I don't know why I always overcompensate. I do it all the time. Thus, the Christmas bills. It is something to think about on another day. Today I am feeling a little homesick, so I have enough on my plate."

I close my spiral notebook and look out the window at our summer garden. I still get so homesick sometimes. Only there is no longer a home, and this is something that my husband and children cannot understand. This kind of homesickness can be very draining. I allow myself to cry a little bit for just a little while, and then I return to what energizes me, the blessings of this simple day.

★★★

Sabbath time creates a kind of solitude for reminiscing about the past. It sits with us as memories rise to the surface of our minds and float by like clouds. Sabbath will tenderly comfort our homesickness and regret. It will allow us time to simply sit with what has gone before. It will allow us to learn something about ourselves, to learn the lessons the past offers us, and then Sabbath will give us the resolve to let go and return to the things that ground us in the present.

If you find yourself looking back at your life today, give yourself permission to dwell there a little while. If you learn something about yourself, do not beat yourself up with this new knowledge. Simply treat it as a souvenir from your former self, and then with intention and mindfulness, return to the present. Anchor your mind in Sabbath time. After all, this moment is the only moment that is real, so allow yourself to be present in it without sadness or regret. Let this moment of Sabbath time bring you to a place of peace with yourself and with others.

## Sunday Dinner Menu

- Ham and Bean Soup
- Spinach Salad with Hot Bacon Dressing
- Banana Cake with Warm Banana Sauce
- Warm Banana Sauce for Cake

## Ham and Bean Soup

### Ingredients

2 (14 1/2-ounce) (435 g) cans of concentrated bean soup
1 cup (250 mL) of water
8 ounces (225 g) of diced precooked ham
1 cup (225 g) of cooked mashed potatoes
1 medium onion, chopped
3 stalks of celery, chopped
3 tablespoons (45 mL) of olive oil
1 teaspoon (4.6 g) of chopped parsley (optional)

### Preparation

Heat olive oil in a small saucepan. Add onion and celery. Cook until onion is translucent and celery is tender.

In a large pot, add bean soup, and dilute with 1 can of water. Mix well. Add ham, onion, celery, and mashed potatoes. Mix well. Simmer for about half an hour. Before serving, add parsley

Serves 6. (Approximately 313 calories per serving.)

Adapted from Mayme Pearson's recipe "Short-Cut US Senate Soup."

# Spinach Salad with Hot Bacon Dressing

## Ingredients

12 ounces (360 g) of baby spinach leaves
6 boiled eggs
8 slices of bacon, reserve fat
1 cup (250 mL) of vinegar
1 tablespoon (14 g) of sugar
Salt and pepper

## Preparation

Place spinach leaves in salad bowl. Slice eggs on top.

Fry bacon, reserving the fat. Cut the bacon into small pieces.

In a saucepan, heat bacon, bacon fat, vinegar, and sugar. Salt and pepper to taste. Mix thoroughly. Pour over salad while warm.

Serves 6. (Approximately 194 calories per serving.)

Adapted from Mayme Pearson's recipe, "Spinach Salad."

# Banana Cake with Warm Banana Sauce

## Ingredients

2 cups (450 g) of brown sugar
3/4 cup (169 g) of shortening
3 cups (675 g) of flour
1 teaspoon (4.6 g) of baking powder
2 teaspoons (9.2 g) of baking soda
2 eggs
6 bananas, mashed
1 teaspoon (5 mL) of vanilla

## Preparation

Preheat oven to 350 degrees F (180 degrees C). Using an electric mixer, cream sugar and shortening. Add eggs, vanilla, and bananas, and beat until well mixed. Add baking powder, baking soda, and flour. Mix until smooth.

Pour batter in a greased, floured 9 × 13–inch cake pan. Bake 30–35 minutes or until a toothpick inserted in middle of cake comes out clean.

# Warm Banana Sauce for Cake

## Ingredients

1 packed cup (225 g) of brown sugar
1/2 cup (125 mL) of milk
3 tablespoons (42 g) of butter or margarine
1 teaspoon of (5 mL) vanilla
1/4 teaspoon (0.5 g) of salt
2 thinly sliced bananas
1/2 cup (120 g) of finely chopped walnuts

## Preparation

In a saucepan over medium heat, mix brown sugar, milk, and butter or margarine. Whisk while cooking until slightly thickened (5–6 minutes). Add vanilla, and cook one more minute. Remove from heat. Fold in bananas and walnuts. Serve while warm over banana cake. Serve with a scoop of vanilla ice cream.

Serves 12. (Approximately 556 calories per serving; includes sauce.)

Adapted from Mayme Pearson's, "Banana Cake."

# SUNDAY #27

# Up at Night

I feel the syncopated tempo in my chest. The sky is jamming. I feel the thunder with its baritone booming and its bass rumbling. I hear the wind wheezing through the spruce pines like Dylan on harmonica. I hear the rain strumming its jazz guitar. Lightening paints the backdrop like a silent artist, stippling the canvas with her jagged brush, painting the horizon a curious shade of yellow, the yellow of faded sunlight, the yellow of a time-worn photograph.

I am sitting in the darkness, a grown woman in her own home. I remember the thunder of childhood storms and the fear that would drive me to the side of my mother's bed. I would sit in the valley of blankets between my parents' legs as Mom propped her pillow against the headboard and smoked a cigarette, its red tip moving like a conductor's baton in the tempest night. And we would sit until the storm subsided, sometimes talking, more often not.

Tonight a deeper fear snaps the thread of sleep, pulling me sharply from a vaporous dream, hours before the alarm clock will startle my husband into Sunday morning. I wake, and I am suffocating, choking on a single thought. Someday I will die. With the thought, there arrives a libretto of things undone, a looking back at life, a cascade of regret that fills my mind drop by drop until I am drowning. The act of rising from my bed is an act of survival.

I've known other nights of terror-filled waking. When a brain tumor claimed a childhood playmate, I woke, worrying that a self-induced headache was a similar cancer claiming my cerebellum. When my father accidentally ran over our little black poodle, Barbette, I woke crying, thinking of the pain and betrayal she endured in that one careless moment. When my cannibalistic guppy drank several of her children in a single gulp, I woke, mourning the brevity and uncertainty of their single small lives. When I opened a magazine on my father's desk and found a photo essay on the Mỹ Lai Massacre, I woke, haunted by the fearful eyes and twisted bodies of people I did not know. When I saw my grandmother's coffin sitting above her grave, I woke, afraid of her feeling cold and of forever looking up through the earth. When my mother began to die at forty-seven years old, passing at fifty-four, I woke and woke and woke until I learned to rise, until I remembered how to rise.

I find it is unpopular, especially in Christian circles, to admit to the fear of death as though the admission nullifies faith and with it, hope. Such an admission gives voice to an uncertainty about what happens the moment after life ceases. It makes the faithful move uncomfortably in their chairs and look about and down with eyes full of avoidance, or it initiates an impassioned defense, so full of Scripture and Dante's visions of heaven and hell that I grow quiet and feel a little bit ashamed for having spoken the truth.

So I've learned to keep the fear of death mostly to myself and mostly from myself, unspoken, pushed below the surface of thought and belief. This is why it lifts its head on stormy nights, rising from the depths of unguarded sleep. Like the Loch Ness Monster surfacing from an ancient sea, it bellows in the darkness to gain my attention.

I have learned that only my tender awareness will quiet the unrest and silence the inner silence of my unspoken fear. This is why I rise and sit quietly as this fearsome teacher roars and weeps. In time, it will grow quiet. In time, my fear will lessen. In time, I will learn to appreciate its presence. I will learn to live fully knowing that I will die. The wisdom of silently rising and patiently waiting is the lesson I learned while sitting with my mother on dark stormy nights.

As I watch the storm soften to rain, I begin to feel sleepy. I walk back to bed, feeling the carpet beneath my bare feet, traversing the night on fragile certainties. Someday I will die. Until that moment, I can cling to my life in despair or embrace it in gratitude. The choice is mine. This is all I can control. My life is connected to everything that was here before I came to be. It is flowing, as it should, into what will come after. My great-grandmother sings in the marrow of my bones. My great-grandchildren dance in the moisture of my mouth, and the divine is at my beginning and at my end. In the deep blue rising of Sunday morning, this is all the faith I can muster.

As I crawl beneath the covers, my husband asks in a voice full of sleep, "Are you okay?"

"I'm fine," I answer, kissing the curve of his shoulder, and I drift toward Sabbath in the warm chrysalis of his back.

★★★

We are all afraid of something. Sometimes a great fear that we cannot fully face or admit will come calling like an unexpected visitor. It will rise from a dream like a ghostly apparition, spring like a demon from the conversation of another, or lumber uninvited into a pleasant memory. Fear can hinder and paralyze, or it can teach. If we cringe and look away, deny and bury, or run and hide, the fear will return again and again. But if we learn to sit quietly without judging ourselves and watch the fear as it moves through our minds, if we allow it to rise and descend without interference, it will lose its hold on us, and it will eventually teach us what it has come to teach.

Sabbath does not give us easy answers and compact explanations. It is not a security blanket. It is a light that beacons from the horizon. It comforts us in the darkness as we rise and as we sit and watch. It remains certain even when we are not as it guides us forever toward a home we cannot articulate.

*Paula Hartman*

## Sunday Dinner Menu

- Upper Crust Chicken
- Homemade Poultry Seasoning
- Asparagus with Soy Sauce
- Mom's Apple Cobbler

---

## Upper Crust Chicken

---

### Ingredients

10 slices of bread
16 ounces (450 g) of chicken, white meat, roasted, sliced into thin pieces
2 cups (450 g) shredded sharp cheddar cheese, divided
1/2 cup (120 g) of mayonnaise
1/2 cup (120 g) of plain Greek yogurt
3 eggs, slightly beaten
1 teaspoon (4.6 g) of salt
1/2 teaspoon (2.3 g) of poultry seasoning (see following recipe)
1 1/2 (375 mL) of milk
1 cup (225 g) of thinly sliced celery

### Preparation

Trim crust from bread, reserving crust. Cut bread slices diagonally into quarters. Cut crusts into cubes. Combine bread cubes, chicken, celery, and 1 3/4 cups of cheese. Mix well.

Spoon the mixture into a rectangular baking dish. Arrange bread quarters over chicken mixture.

In a mixing bowl, combine mayonnaise, yogurt, eggs, and seasonings. Mix well. Gradually add milk, mixing until blended. Pour over bread.

Sprinkle with remaining cheese. Cover. Refrigerate several hours or overnight.

Bake uncovered at 375 degrees F (190 degrees C) for 30 minutes.

Serves 6. (Approximately 443 calories per serving.)

Adapted from Chris Bryte's "Upper Crust Chicken."

## Homemade Poultry Seasoning

### Ingredients

2 teaspoons (9.2 g) of ground sage
1 teaspoon (4.6 g) of ground thyme
1/2 teaspoon (2.3 g) of ground marjoram
1/2 teaspoon (2.3 g) of ground rosemary
1/4 teaspoon (1.2 g) of ground nutmeg
1/4 teaspoon (1.2 g) of ground black pepper
1/8 teaspoon (0.5 g) of onion powder

### Preparation

Combine all ingredients, and mix well. Place in a jelly jar or used spice bottle. Cover. Label, and store with other spices.

Makes 10 1/2 teaspoon servings. (Approximately 1.4 calories per serving.)

From Mayme Pearson's, "Poultry Seasoning".

## Asparagus with Soy Sauce

### Ingredients

1 bunch of asparagus (approximately 2 dozen spears, washed)
4 tablespoons (60 mL) of soy sauce
Parchment paper

### Preparation

Trim tough ends from the asparagus spears. Place the asparagus evenly on a sheet of parchment paper. Drizzle soy sauce on the asparagus. Fold the parchment paper into a packet around the asparagus, and seal edges. Place on a cooking sheet. Cook at 350 degrees F (180 degrees C) for 20–25 minutes.

Makes 6 servings. (Approximately 45 calories per serving.)

Adapted from Patrick Conry's "Asparagus."

# Mom's Apple Cobbler

## Ingredients

1 cup (225 g) of sugar
1 cup (225 g) of flour
1 egg
1/2 teaspoon (2.3 g) of baking powder
1 stick (240 g) of margarine, softened
1 (24-ounce) (720 g) can of apple pie filling
Sugar for sprinkling on top of cobbler

## Preparation

Cream the sugar and margarine. Add sugar, flour, and baking powder. Mix well. Place fruit in the bottom of a greased, square baking pan. Put batter on top of fruit. Sprinkle the dough with sugar.

Bake at 375 degrees F (190 degrees C) for 20–25 minutes until crust is well browned or until a toothpick inserted in center comes out clean.

Serve with vanilla ice cream.

Serves 8. (Approximately 583 calories per serving.)

Adapted from Polly Hensley's "Fruit Cobbler."

SUNDAY #28

# Just Watching the Garden Grow

Our vegetable garden is my sanctuary from the everyday routine of the week. Here I don't wear shoes. Here the wind sings a hymn of praise as it runs like a child through the grass. Birds sing soprano from the pin oaks along the fence line. I sing along with abandon because there is no one to annoy, except my fledgling plants, and they don't complain much. My favorite gardening hymn is the theme song from *Green Acres*. I sing it with great enthusiasm. I also sing it with a Hungarian accent in just the right places. I feel no embarrassment. There is little need for pretense or propriety while sitting in the dirt.

In this little garden in my own backyard, I learn from quiet teachers who do not lecture or cajole, teachers who simply teach by example, by existing, by growing slowly into what they were created to be. Here I learn that planting gourds beside the beans is not wise. Gourds have poor manners and will not stay on their side of the garden. They vine wildly, weaving into and climbing onto the beans plants that seem to be saying, "Mom, he's touching me!" Searching for beans beneath the jungle of wide leaves teaches me the need for boundaries and spacing.

In the garden I learn to let freshly tilled ground sit for a few days before planting because the flock of birds that descends on it to eat the newly exposed worms and grubs will also eat the corn seed. I learn that rushing to plant creates a period of futile waiting. The replanting teaches me patience and the benefits of trying again.

In this garden I learn that my husband and I have differing approaches to the art of planting corn and beans. If left alone, I eye

200

the rows, happy if they are relatively straight. I space the seed using my feet and calculate the depth of planting with my thumb. My husband uses a ruler, a retractable tape measure, rolls of string, stakes, and a detailed gardening manual. For me, the garden is a place to think and work in the sunshine. For him, it is a wilderness to be conquered. We compromise. The garden is staked and strung in perfectly measured rows, but we use our feet to measure the earth and space the seed.

Watching the garden grow, I learn that too little rain is not good for the garden. Nor is too much rain, especially when there is a lot of clay in the soil, which causes the water to form deep puddles around the tomato plants, drowning them. I learn that rain can fall softly or fall with such force that it beats the plants, bending and breaking them. I learn that the gardener has absolutely no control over how much or how little rain falls just as she has no control over many other things in her life. I learn to do the best I can and accept the fact that the perfect conditions will probably never come along.

But I am not weeding or fertilizing today. I am just resting in the grass, watching the garden grow, allowing my soul to stretch in the sunshine. Small stalks of green promise corn. Fragile yellow flowers hold the template for zucchini. Vines spiral and climb, bracing themselves to bear tomatoes. This is a place of renewal and hope, a place of gently becoming. Looking into a sky full of blue, I begin a hymn of praise, "Green Acres is the place to be."

★★★

Sabbath teaches us to recognize the sacred in the ordinary, to find sanctuaries in unexpected places, such as in a summer garden, on a quiet bench near a city street, or in a shaft of sunlight pouring over a windowsill. Sabbath insists that we find a quiet place to just sit for a while and watch the world and its spinning, to do much of nothing, to simply be. Actually, Sabbath mandates the practice of sitting. Only when we are still do we begin to pay attention to what we have been given. Only when we are still do we learn to recognize that the spirit of Sabbath is sitting with us like a very old friend on a quiet summer porch. Only when we are still do we learn to rise with humility and become a sanctuary for others.

## Sunday Dinner Menu

- Macaroni Salad with Chicken
- Herbed Tomato-Cucumber Platter
- Curried Eggs
- Strawberry Surprise

---

## Macaroni Salad with Chicken

---

### Ingredients

8 ounces (240 g) of elbow macaroni, cooked and chilled
3 cups (675 g) diced chicken, white meat, roasted
1 1/2 cup (345 g) diced celery
1 cup (225 g) diced sweet pickle
1 cup (225 g) mayonnaise
1/4 cup (56g) minced parsley
6 stuffed olives, sliced for garnish

### Preparation

Mix all ingredients except olives. Toss and chill. Garnish with sliced olives. Serve with crackers.

Serves 6. (Approximately 412 calories per serving.)

Adapted from Mayme Pearson's "Macaroni Salad."

# Herbed Tomato-Cucumber Platter

## Ingredients

3 large ripe tomatoes, peeled and sliced
3 large cucumbers, sliced and peeled
1 1/2 (6.9 g) teaspoons of salt
1 1/2 teaspoons (6.9 g) of freshly ground pepper
2 teaspoons (9.2 g) of dill seed
1 teaspoon (4.6 g) of snipped parsley
1/2 cup (125 mL) of olive oil
3 tablespoons (45 mL) of wine vinegar

## Preparation

In a small bowl, combine salt, pepper, dill seed, parsley, oil, and vinegar. Mix well. Layer tomato slices at one side of large shallow dish, drizzling each layer with part of seasoned oil and vinegar. Repeat with cucumber on the other side. Chill several hours. Occasionally spoon the dressing over tomatoes and cucumbers.

Serves 8. (Approximately 138 calories per serving.)

Adapted from Mayme Pearson's "Herbed Vegetable Platter."

*Paula Hartman*

## Curried Eggs

**Ingredients**

8 boiled eggs
1 teaspoon (4.6 g) of curry powder
1/4 teaspoon (1.2 g) of salt
1/4 cup (56 g) of soft margarine
2 tablespoons (28 g) of mayonnaise
1 tablespoon (15 mL) of lemon juice

**Preparation**

Cut eggs in half. Place yolks into a bowl, and place the whites on a serving plate. Cream egg yolks, curry powder, salt, margarine, mayonnaise, and lemon juice. Stuff egg whites with egg yolk mixture, and refrigerate until serving.

Serves 16. (Approximately 64 calories per serving.)

Adapted from Mayme Pearson's "Curried Eggs."

# Strawberry Surprise

## Ingredients

1 pint (450 g) of fresh strawberries
1/4 (56 g) cup of sugar
1 box of yellow cake mix
1 egg
Milk (amount determined by instructions on cake mix)
2 (4 1/2-ounce) (135 g) boxes of strawberry instant pudding
2 (8-ounce) (240 g) packages of cream cheese
1 (16-ounce) (450 g) container of frozen whipped cream, thawed
1 cup (225 g) of fresh strawberries for garnish

## Preparation

Wash strawberries. Reserve five or six strawberries for garnish. Remove tops, and slice into a bowl. Sprinkle with sugar, and set aside.

Prepare cake mix as directed on box. Use milk to replace water, and add one additional egg. Pour batter into a 10 × 15–inch pan. Bake as directed. Cool.

When cake is cool, prepare pudding as directed. Beat cream cheese into pudding. Spread this mixture on cake.

Spoon the fresh strawberries over the pudding. Frost with whipped cream. Garnish with strawberry halves. Refrigerate.

Serves 12. (Approximately 386 calories per serving.)

Adapted from Connie Beery's recipe "Strawberry Surprise"

# The Zen of Weeding

Again and again, I've tried to learn the art of meditation. Well, short of finding a yogi or spending my summer vacation at an ashram. I've read a plethora of books on the subject, all instructing me to stop reading about meditation and to start practicing meditation. I've listened to a multitude of audiotapes. I've tried to relax at the direction of many a calm and soothing voice, describing seashores and peaceful gardens, encouraging me to pay attention to my breath. Then I wake up startled and realize that once again I have fallen asleep in an attempt to meditate.

Once I went on a day retreat led by a young pastor who promised to teach a group of adventurous Methodists the art of contemplative meditation. Although I was eager to learn the art, I nearly gave myself whiplash by lunchtime as I slipped into a deep sleep and then snapped awake, jarring my neck. At the end of the day, the pastor sent us into the woods to meditate alone for one hour. "Be still and know that I am God." I found a beautiful spot beneath a grove of pine trees. I sat down on a blanket of brown needles. I stretched out on my back and watched the rhythm of green braches skimming the breeze. I began following my breath as instructed. I woke up half an hour later with pinecone embedded in my face and a strange bug crawling up my left nostril.

I have learned instead to weed the garden. Weeding the garden seems to accomplish a great deal of what meditation promises. For me, weeding is a form of physical meditation, similar I suppose to Tai Chi, only my hands and knees are in the dirt. The simple, almost rhythmic movement of gripping and pulling connects me to a deep place where my mind can be still. Something in that stillness teaches me who I am. I do not need lengthy instructions. I do not need to analyze what I am doing. I merely need to show up at the garden's edge and begin.

Some weeds come out of the earth easily. They slip from the ground with straight, long roots. These are my favorites, and I sometimes hold them up in amazement like a fisherman with a seven-pound bass. Other weeds are deep with roots that branch and grip. I must work to loosen them before they will let go of the soil. These give me calluses and blisters, and they make my hands stronger. Some weeds have a built-in defense system of microscopic prickles or tiny thorns. These weeds fight back. I've learned to approach them gingerly and with due respect, greatly reducing occurrences of personal injury. Other weeds are actually attractive, bearing delicate flowers or intricate leaves, ground cover simply growing in the wrong place. I pull these as well, understanding that even things of apparent beauty can strangle and injure the real growth of a garden.

I pull the weeds with a degree of restraint. If I tug too hard, I simply tear the head from the root, and the weed will quickly regrow. If I do not watch what I am doing, I pull the weed and find a flower or infant vegetable plant attached to it. I've learned that while it is important to remove what chokes and crowds, the work must be done tenderly and with thought to avoid injuring something newly growing in the same soil.

As I weed, I simply breathe and allow my mind to wander from thought to thought, never lingering. The wind strokes my hair like an affectionate grandmother. I swat away a small fly with teeth like a pit bull, and soon he is forgotten. I allow memories to float by like the clouds overhead, recognized but full of misty nothingness.

My son—and all the contradictions of being seventeen—walks to the garden's edge and stretches out on the grass. He talks to me while I work, his talk full of the yearning to be grown. Our dog, Molly, puts her nose into my ear and then lies down beside my son to keep watch. I just keep pulling and pulling, one weed after another ... after another ... after another.

Today I have no need for soothing voices or imaginary gardens. I have a new blister and several fresh bug bites. My knees and hands are embedded with dirt. I am grass-stained, scratched, sweaty, tired, and totally awake. Small green tomatoes are rising from fragile flowers. The little boy who used to ride my hip has gone in the house to shave before his girlfriend arrives to spend the evening. I will follow in a moment and sit in the porch swing, drinking cold, sweet tea. But first, I pause to breathe a prayer of gratitude for what is growing in this place, for the lessons learned and the uncertainties endured, for what challenges me and what nourishes me, and for the weeds within and the weeds without.

★★★

There are many activities that might be considered work, yet when riding tandem with a long Sabbath afternoon, these can transform themselves into a quiet place to think, drift, and dream—washing dishes by hand with white soapy bubbles and warm water or sewing with the rhythmic rise and fall of the needle, the strands of thread held in tension.

Routine tasks can engage and renew us if they are done with care and gratitude, with a sense of privilege, not obligation. Find such an activity today, and lose yourself in it for a little while. Let your mind unwind. Find the pulse, and the play in the work. Recall the pleasant dignity that comes from this kind of modest work. Know that even the simplest endeavor can teach deep lessons and serve as a gateway to the divine.

# Sunday Dinner Menu

- Chicken and Rice Casserole
- Layered Lettuce Salad
- Turtle Cake

---

## Chicken and Rice Casserole

---

### Ingredients

2 tablespoons (30 mL) of olive oil
1 small onion
1/4 (56 g) of French-cut carrots
5 cloves of minced garlic
3 cups (675 g) of cooked chicken breast
1/4 cup (56 g) of vegetable broth or water
3 cups (675 g) of cooked whole-wheat spaghetti
1/3 cup (83 mL) of soy sauce

### Preparation

Cut chicken into small pieces. Cook spaghetti until al dente. Set both aside.

In a medium-sized skillet, heat olive oil. Add onion and carrots. Cook until the onion is translucent and carrots are tender. Add garlic, and cook 2 more minutes

Add vegetable oil and chicken breast. Simmer for 10 minutes.

Add spaghetti and soy sauce. Mix well.

Serves 6. (Approximately 306 calories per serving.)

From the kitchen of Paula Hartman.

# Layered Lettuce Salad

## Ingredients

1 head of lettuce, washed and torn into pieces
1 green pepper, chopped
1 small sweet onion, halved and thinly sliced
4–5 stalks of celery, thinly sliced
6–8 slices of bacon, fried crisp and chopped into small pieces
4 hard-boiled eggs, sliced
1 cup (225 g) of halved cherry tomatoes
1 cup (225 g) of cauliflower florets
1 cup (225 g) of broccoli florets
1 1/2 cups (345 g) of mayonnaise
1 cup (225 g) of shredded mild cheddar cheese

## Preparation

Place torn lettuce into an oblong dish. Layer vegetables, bacon, eggs, etc. Spread mayonnaise on top, and sprinkle with cheddar cheese. Refrigerate for at least 12 hours before serving.

Add or omit fresh vegetables as desired. Fresh mushrooms and frozen peas may also be included.

Serves 8. (Approximately 290 calories per serving.)

Adapted from Mary Havenar's recipe, "Layered Lettuce."

# Turtle Cake

## Ingredients

1 German chocolate cake mix
1 (16-ounce) (450 g) package of caramels, unwrapped
1/2 cup (125 mL) of evaporated milk
3/4 cup (191 g) of butter or margarine
1 (12-ounce) (360 g) package of chocolate chips
1/2 cup (120 g) of peanuts or pecans

## Preparation

Preheat oven to 350 degrees (180 degrees C).

Mix German chocolate cake mix per instructions. Pour 1/2 bowl of batter into a greased 9 × 13–inch pan. Bake at 350 degrees F (180 degrees C) for 15 minutes.

Meanwhile, place caramels in a saucepan. Add evaporated milk and butter or margarine. Pour over cake.

Sprinkle chocolate chips and nuts over caramel mixture.

Top with the remaining cake batter. Bake at 350 degrees F (180 degrees C) for 20–25 minutes. Serve with whipped cream.

Serves 16. (Approximately 393 calories per serving; includes 2 tablespoons [30 g] of whipped cream per serving.)

Adapted from Shirley Spencer's recipe "Turtle Cake."

## SUNDAY #30

# Remembrance

Our pastor speaks quiet words of remembrance as the faithful wait in line to receive Communion. "The body and blood of Christ, given for you, Mark," he says as my sixteen-year-old son tears a piece of bread from the split loaf, dips it in the chalice of grape juice, and kneels at the altar rail.

As I step forward to receive the elements, I see that my son is holding a piece of Communion bread large enough to make a sandwich. From the corner of my eye, I watch him stuff the entire piece of bread into his mouth and begin to chew. My son knows that I am watching him and that I am trying to ignore his obvious delight at my discomfort. As I kneel beside him, he is still chewing. And being the mother of impropriety, I take a deep breath to stifle the laughter rising in my throat and pause to remember.

I remember another Communion Sunday. I was twelve years old. My father, robed in black, was blessing the elements. He was the only minister I had ever known. I knew the words he spoke by heart, "And on that last night with the twelve, he took the bread in his hands and he broke it, saying, 'This brokenness, I share with you.'"

Outside the morning was frigid. The trees were thick with ice, and the brown grass was frozen straight. Although our parsonage stood a stone's throw from our white cinder-block church, the walk across the slick terrain had been slow and difficult in our patent-leather shoes. My dad had scattered rock salt on the sidewalk, and he had tried to hack the ice from the cement stairs with a show shovel; however, the ice had not loosened its grip.

The faithful were forced to mount the stairs on unreliable feet, clinging to one another's hands, arms, and clothing. Judging by the sparse assembly, many had chosen to remain at home where they were safe and warm with hips and skulls intact. The wind cut at the stained glass windows and crept through the molding, making the sanctuary cold. I was sitting beside my mother and my sister.

We do not know the why of what occurred next. We only know that it occurred. At our family table, where the best of family tales were perfected in the telling and retelling, what occurred started the story "The Day Dad Nearly Choked to Death on the Body of Jesus."

After Dad raised the loaf of bread above his head, saying, "Accept the brokenness of our Lord in remembrance of his love for you." Dad then tore a piece of bread from the loaf. It was a large piece too, one the size of a dinner roll or a hamburger bun. And without one inkling of forethought, not one, he crammed the entire hunk of bread into his mouth, and he began to chew and chew and chew. And chew. A hush fell over the faithful as they watched and waited, wondering if their pastor was ever going to stop chewing and swallow.

In the silence of that waiting and wondering, my mother whispered loudly, "He is going to choke to death." She might as well have been using a microphone because nearly everyone heard her. The faithful started shifting in their seats, smiling at one another. Dad kept chewing.

He chewed and chewed and chewed. He smiled apologetically, and he chewed. And he chewed. He simply could not swallow the lump of soggy bread in his mouth. It was if the yeast and the gluten had taken on lives of their own, growing and swelling beneath his palate.

As was usual in these types of situations, my dad's devoted wife of thirteen years and four children began to laugh. At first, it was a silent, shoulder-shaking chuckle, but it quickly became a barely audible huffy, puffy kind of laugh that sounded like a cat hacking up a fur ball. Knowing his wife all too well, my dad shot her a look that said, "Please don't." This ended all possible hope of restraint. Mom began to laugh in earnest. She threw her head back, laughing until forced to dig through her purse for a tissue. Her laughter floated through the sanctuary like nitrous oxide, infecting the faithful like a contagion.

Suddenly my dad stopped chewing. He looked at the faithful, his expression one of desperate determination, and he swallowed. Hard. Painfully hard. The laughter stopped immediately. Dad's face grew red. He leaned forward, placing his palms on the Communion table. The faithful held their collective breath. I like to think that the ever-vigilant Dr. Peters was perched on the edge of his pew, fully prepared to bolt down the aisle and thrust Dad against the organ in a Heimlich maneuver to remove the host from his throat.

Dad took a deep breath, obviously relieved, and in a somewhat raspy voice, he began to once again speak familiar words. "There is brokenness in life, but there is also healing." Dad held the chalice above his head and continued, "This cup will heal you and make you whole. Accept the mercy of our Lord in remembrance of his love for you." Then Dad smiled, and the faithful smiled in return. "My friends," he said, "come. The table is prepared for you." That was Dad's forte, grace under pressure.

My mother loved to tell this story. She would tell it at Christmas, at Thanksgiving, anytime and to anyone new at our table. And we kids relished hearing it. At one telling Dad chewed for a full forty-five minutes.

My father's grandson is kneeling beside me, resting his forehead against his folded hands. He is sixteen, straining toward thirty. And he is still chewing.

★★★

The Sabbath invites us to the table of grace. It allows us to share in the brokenness of humankind and reminds us of the love that longs to make us whole. Sabbath prepares a holy meal to which all are invited. We need not prove our worthiness or list our accomplishments. The invitation is not based on merit. It is a gift.

Pause today, and allow yourself to experience grace. Accept that your Creator understands who you are and accepts you. Accept that you are fully known and fully loved. You do not need to do anything else. Simply rest in the peace of this acceptance, and allow the spirit of Sabbath to nourish you, heal you, and make you whole.

# Sunday Dinner Menu

- Cheese-Stuffed Pasta Shells
- Cucumber Salad
- French Bread
- Pineapple Cake

## Cheese-Stuffed Pasta Shells

### Ingredients

1 pound (450 g) of large pasta shells
3 tablespoons (42 g) of margarine
1/4 cup onion, finely chopped
1 (10-ounce) (300 g) box of frozen spinach, drained
8 ounces (240 g) of cheddar cheese, shredded
4 ounces (120 g) of Colby cheese, shredded
1 (24-ounce) (720 g) container of cottage cheese
1 (32-ounce) (960 g) jar of spaghetti sauce
2 eggs

### Preparation

Preheat oven to 375 degrees F (190 degrees C).

Melt butter. Mix with onion, and spread in the bottom of a 9 × 13–inch baking pan. Place in oven for 10–15 minutes, allowing the onions to soften. When done, remove from oven.

Meanwhile, drain spinach. Cook shells according to package directions. Drain and allow the dish to cool for a bit.

In a mixing bowl, mix drained spinach, eggs, cottage cheese, cheddar cheese, and Colby cheese together with a fork.

*Paula Hartman*

Fill each cooked shell with a tablespoon of the cheese mixture. Place in the pan containing butter or margarine and onions. Form a single layer in the pan. Pour spaghetti sauce over shells. Bake at 375 degrees F (190 degrees C) for 30 minutes.

Serving size: 2 shells. (Approximately 352 calories per serving.)

Adapted from Noreen Cogar's recipe, "Stuffed Shells."

# Cucumber Salad

## Ingredients

2 medium cucumbers, peeled
1 medium onion, thinly sliced
1 1/4 (5.8 g) teaspoons of salt
1 cup (225 g) of sour cream
2 tablespoons (30 mL) of vinegar
1/4 teaspoon (1.2 g) of sugar
1/8 teaspoon (0.5 g) of paprika
1 tablespoon (14 g) of parsley flakes

## Preparation

Draw tines of fork lengthwise down cucumbers. Then cut into thin slices. Add onion and sprinkle with 1 teaspoon of salt. Let stand for 10 minutes. Drain. In a separate bowl, mix sour cream, remaining salt, vinegar, sugar, paprika, and parsley flakes. Add sour cream mixture to cucumbers, mixing lightly with a fork. Chill thoroughly. Makes 2 cups.

Serves 6. (Approximately 105 calories per serving.)

Adapted from Sandy Bridenthal's recipe "Cucumbers in Sour Cream."

# French Bread

## Ingredients

2 1/2 cups (500 mL) of warm water (not hot)
2 packages of active dry yeast
1 tablespoon (14 g) of salt
1 tablespoon (14 g) of margarine
7 cups (1.6 kg) of flour
Cornmeal
1 egg white
1 tablespoon (15 mL) of cold water

## Preparation

Pour warm water (105–115 degrees F) into a large, warm bowl. Sprinkle yeast over the water, and stir until dissolved. Add salt and margarine. Add flour slowly, and stir until flour is well blended. The dough will be sticky. Place the dough in a greased bowl. Cover with a dish-towel.

Let rise in a warm place that's free from draft until doubled in bulk (about 1 hour).

Turn dough onto a lightly floured board. Divide into 2 equal portions. Roll each into an oblong 15 × 10–inch rectangle. Beginning at the wide side of dough, roll each half up tightly. Seal edges by pinching the dough together at the seam. Taper ends by rolling gently back and forth.

Place loaves on a greased baking sheet sprinkled with cornmeal. Cover. Again, let rise in a warm place that's free from drafts until doubled in bulk (about 1 hour).

With a sharp knife, make diagonal cuts of top of each load. Bake at 450 degrees F (230 degrees C) for 25 minutes. Remove from oven and brush with egg white mixed with cold water. Return to oven. Bake 5 minutes longer.

Serving: 1 (1 1/2-ounce) slice of bread. (Approximately 281 calories per serving.)

Adapted from June Floyd's recipe "French Bread."

# Pineapple Cake

## Ingredients

1 1/2 (345 g) cups of sugar
2 cups (450 g) of flour
2 eggs
1 teaspoon (4.6 g) of soda
1 teaspoon (4.6 g) of salt
1 cup (225 g) of crushed pineapple, juice included
1 cup (225 g) of brown sugar
1 cup (225 g) of chopped nuts

## Topping for Pineapple Cake

3/4 cup (168 g) of sugar
1 small can of evaporated milk
1 1/2 sticks (180 g) of butter or margarine
1 teaspoon (5 mL) of vanilla

## Preparation

In a large mixing bowl, whisk sugar and eggs until well blended. Add flour, soda, salt, and crushed pineapple with juice. Mix well. Pour into a greased and floured 9 × 12–inch baking pan. In a separate small bowl, mix brown sugar and nuts. Sprinkle over batter. Bake at 350 degrees F (180 degrees C) for 30–35 minutes or until a toothpick inserted in the middle of the cake comes out clean. Let cool.

On stovetop, bring 3/4 cup of sugar, evaporated milk, butter or margarine, and vanilla to a boil. While hot, pour over cake.

Serve with whipped cream.

Serves 12. (Approximately 574 calories per serving; includes topping and 2 tablespoons (25 mL) of whipped cream.)

Adapted from Jo Kelly's recipe "Granny Cake."

# SUNDAY #31

# Letting Go

The days are growing shorter. The crisp air of autumn skips briskly through the last days of summer. The stores are stocked with back-to-school supplies. "Look," I tell my daughter Emily, "crayons in new metallic shades. You know, all of your friends are going to have these."

"Okay, Mom," Emily replies. "Put the crayons in the cart." She is humoring me, but I don't care. I know she no longer needs back-to-school crayons. I know she needs a graphing calculator and folders without cute little animals, teen idols, or superheroes on the front. I know she needs college-ruled notebook paper and mechanical pencils. I just don't like it.

I pick up a bottle of white paste. "How about some of this?" I ask. "What for?"

"To paste stuff."

"Like what?"

"Stuff. You know, stuff."

She takes the paste and deliberately replaces it on the shelf. "No paste," she says.

"Then how about one of these little school boxes for your desk?" I ask. "Oh, look at this one, hologram fish."

"Mom, are you okay?"

"Yes," I answer in a pitiful little tone, dropping my head. (This is a tactic I've used for years to get my own way. Of course, the kids are catching on, so the chances of it working are only about fifty-fifty.) "I just thought you might like to buy a school box for old times' sake."

"Oh, all right," Emily answers. "I'll get school box if it will make you happy, but I get to choose the one I want." I love the way she indulges me while also maintaining some degree of autonomy.

I am not having a breakdown. Nor am I regressing to some earlier period in my life. I'm just playing. I am earnestly trying to ignore the blue mood that crawled out of bed with me this morning—a blueness that seems to be swelling like a tick with its head beneath my skin, feeding on the realization that after Emily rejects safety scissors and a pink backpack with stripes that glow in the dark, we will need to purchase sheets, bath towels, and an iron. Emily is leaving for college.

I am trying to be upbeat, trying to create a pleasant memory, but inside, I am acutely aware that summer is nearly over. The bloodsucking blueness seems to be coming in waves, building in intensity like labor pains. How do you prepare yourself to let go? How do you turn and leave your child in a strange new place, knowing the she is afraid?

When my mother was ill and growing closer to death, I saved my vacation time and kept my schedule loose, anticipating the call from my sister telling me, "It won't be long." I imagined driving home. I imagined long days and longer nights of lingering while Mom died in a haze of Thorazine. I pictured myself holding my mother's hand as she passed from this place to another.

I was making grilled cheese sandwiches when the call came. My father spoke slowly with forced restraint, his voice quiet and calm. "Sweetheart, your mother died this morning." I was stunned. For seven years I watched my mother let go of her life piece by piece. For seven years I prepared myself for her death, thinking of that final moment and the moment after. But the moment didn't arrive as I had imagined. I stood in silent disbelief in my own kitchen, wondering what I should do next, wondering how she simply slipped away one Sunday morning when no one was looking, wondering how a mother finds the courage to let go, knowing her child is afraid?

My feet and legs are tired from walking the mall. I still need to pack lunches for work on Monday and throw a load of laundry into the washer. Then Emily plops down beside me on the couch. "I'm not going out tonight," she says. "Do you want to watch a movie?"

"I'm really tired, honey, and there's a bunch of stuff I need to do," I reply.

"Mommy, you're going to miss me when I'm far, far away," she says in a pitiful tone, dropping her head. This a manipulative maneuver she learned from her mother, only she pushes her bottom lip ever-so-slightly forward, taking the ploy to a new level. And calling me Mommy is brilliant, simply brilliant.

Suddenly, she is three, refusing to hold my hand on a department store escalator. She is pulling, and I am afraid my holding on will make her pull harder and cause her to fall. So she agrees to stand very still, unaware of my hand gripping the hood of her coat.

She is five, and we are walking into Lincoln Way Elementary School. She carries a new box of crayons and a pair of pink safety scissors in the *My Pretty Pony* backpack. She becomes timid as we reach the door of her kindergarten classroom, but she hesitates for only a moment as her new teacher says hello. She waves at me, and I wave back. She does not know that I stand in the doorway and watch until I am sure she is okay, before I walk to the car and cry.

She is eleven, and we are packing her gear for a weeklong trip to summer camp. She has been to camp before, but never alone. She packs a deck of cards and her teddy bear. She is afraid that she won't make new friends or that she'll feel homesick. I pack bug spray, sunscreen, a flashlight, and a warm jacket. I want her to have what she needs to feel warm, safe, and fearless.

And she is sixteen, and we are driving down Hubbard Valley Road. She is driving, and I am sitting in the passenger seat. She clutches the steering wheel as we ride the edge of the road, going barely twenty-five miles per hour. I encourage her to go just a little faster, and she speeds up as I grip the edge of my seat. She does not know that I will spend the next two years sitting by the window, watching for her headlights.

I have been saying good-bye to this child in increments since the day she was born. College is just one more small good-bye. There will be others.

I know that at each moment of letting go there will also be a time of lingering. I will remain near until I know she is okay. She may not be aware of my presence, but I will be there, wrapped in paper care packages, tucked into favorite recipes, kissing her hair through telephone wires, embracing her with letters and birthday cards, protecting her with prayers. And when the distance grows too great, I will hide in the sunlight that falls across her bedroom floor, and I will paint a rainbow of light on her walls. In truth, a mother never lets go.

We are sharing a blanket and bowl of popcorn. Emily is leaning against my shoulder as the music rises. Life feels sacred and precious and brief. I am fighting tears. And my own mother is lingering near me.

★★★

A lifetime is an incremental lesson in letting go. The privilege of loving deeply, of embracing life fully, and of living long and well bears the unavoidable toll of relinquishment. At times we let go in order to move forward. We release our grip on what we hold dear to create the freedom necessary for growth and maturity.

At other times we let go under duress, releasing our grip against our will, mourning lost aspects of ourselves, parting with people we love, leaving places we long to remain, railing against the passage of time and the uncertainty of growing older.

Sabbath does not judge. Instead it grants us permission to drop our guard, permission to cast off shells of stoicism, permission to be honest with ourselves. Sabbath allows us the time we need to weep if we need to weep, to scream if we need to scream, to plan what can be planned, to say what needs to be said, and to garner strength and wisdom for what lies ahead. And then it takes the reins from our hands and allows us to rest and breathe in the holiness of here and now.

Today, take some time to honestly contemplate the next phase of your life. The rewards of such reflection can be useful, but be gentle with yourself. Ask the spirit of Sabbath to grant you enough strength and wisdom to embrace life fully, to live each day passionately, and to love deeply, even as you are letting go year by year, day by day, and hour by hour. Then rest, trusting that when the time of letting go arrives, you will have sufficient courage and divine help. And always remember that you will not be alone.

# Sunday Dinner Menu

- Deluxe Burgers with Tomatoes
- Cabbage Salad
- Dressing for Cabbage Salad
- Best Cheesy Potatoes Ever
- Banana Nut Bread

---

## Deluxe Burgers with Tomatoes

---

### Ingredients

1 pound (450 g) of lean hamburger
1 small onion, diced
1/2 green pepper, diced
1/2 cup (120 g) of finely crushed crackers
1 egg, slightly beaten
2 (15-ounce) (450 g) cans of diced tomatoes with juice
4 ounces (125 mL) of tomato juice
1/2 cup (120 g) of cheddar cheese

### Preparation

Preheat oven to 350 degrees F (180 degrees C).

In a mixing bowl, mix hamburger, onion, green pepper, crackers, and eggs. Mix well. Form into eight patties.

In a large skillet on medium heat, cook hamburger patties 4–5 minutes on each side.

When browned, place patties in a baking dish. Cover with tomatoes and tomato juice. Bake for 30 minutes. Remove from oven. Sprinkle with cheese, and return to oven for another 10 minutes or until the cheese is melted.

Serves 8. (Approximately 220 calories per 6-ounce serving.)

From the kitchen of Paula Hartman.

# Cabbage Salad

## Ingredients

16 ounces (450 g) of cabbage, raw
2 carrots,
1/2 green pepper

## Preparation

Mix cabbage, carrots, and peppers in a bowl.

# Dressing for Cabbage Salad

## Ingredients

1 1/2 (45 mL) tablespoons of lemon juice
4 tablespoons (60 g) of sugar (or to taste)
8 tablespoons (120 g) of sour cream
salt and pepper to taste

## Preparation

Mix well. Pour over cabbage, and mix thoroughly. Chill.

Serves 6. (Approximately 97 calories per serving; includes dressing.)

Adapted from Mayme Pearson's "Cabbage Salad."

# Best Cheesy Potatoes Ever

## Ingredients

8 or 9 red potatoes, cooked and grated with skins
1/2 pound (125 g) of grated sharp cheddar cheese
1 teaspoon (4.6 g) of mustard
1 1/2 teaspoons (6.9 g) of salt
1/2 pint (250 mL) of whipping cream
1 cup (250 mL) of milk
1/8 teaspoon (0.5 g) of nutmeg

## Preparation

Cook potatoes, and grate into a buttered casserole dish. In a saucepan, heat cheese, mustard, salt, milk, whipping cream, and nutmeg until cheese is melted. Pour over potatoes. Sprinkle with paprika on top. Bake at 325 degrees F (160 degrees) for 1 hour.

Serves 12. (Approximately 298 calories per serving.)

Adapted from Jo Kelly's recipe "Potato Casserole."

# Banana Nut Bread

## Ingredients

2 cups (450 g) of white sugar
1/2 cup (120 g) of margarine
1/2 cup (120 g) of unsweetened applesauce
4 beaten eggs
2 cups (450 g) of flour
1 teaspoon (4.6 g) of salt
2 teaspoons (9.2 g) of baking soda
2 cups (450 g) of mashed ripe bananas
1/2 cup (120 g) of crushed walnuts

## Preparation

In a large mixing bowl, cream the sugar and margarine. Mix in the applesauce and eggs.

In a separate mixing bowl, add flour, salt, and baking soda. Mix well. Add to wet mixture. Mix well.

Add banana, and mix well. Fold in walnuts.

Place batter into two greased 9 × 5–inch loaf pans. Bake at 350 degrees F (180 degrees C) for 60–70 minutes. A toothpick inserted into middle should come out clean.

Serves 12. (Approximately 343 calories per serving.)

From the kitchen of Paula Hartman.

## IN CONCLUSION

# Thinking about Walt Whitman

This morning I read a magazine article about Walt Whitman. The author said that Walt Whitman's brain was donated to science and that that it is rumored that a lab tech accidentally dropped the brilliant brain on the floor and that it had to be discarded. Reading this, I laughed out loud. I could only imagine what went through that poor tech's mind.

The article also spoke about how Whitman found his poetry in common people and common things. I think the older we get, the more we find common people and common things poetic. I think of a recent trip I took to visit a friend in West Virginia. Joe is seventy-eight years old. He was born into the poverty that is Appalachia. He has done a lot of living. We have become fast friends.

Joe's house has no air-conditioning, so we spent most of the visit sitting on his front porch, appreciating the breeze, and listening to the lovely sound of Sugar Creek rushing by. As we sat there talking, a doe and her fawn walked from the woods. As the mother deer ate apples from underneath Joe's apple trees, her fawn began to run in wide, joyous circles, leaping into the air, running for the sheer fun of running. It was a lovely thing to watch. I like to think that Walt Whitman would have enjoyed it and might have even been inspired to scribble a few lines in a notebook.

Whitman chose to write about the joyous things in life. Knowing that joy is less common than sorrow, I try to follow his lead. When I put my fingers on the keyboard, I do my best to focus on the things that bring me joy.

I hope this romp through Sabbath time has reaffirmed the things in your life that bring you joy. I hope you feel refreshed. I hope you feel less alone as you navigate your complicated life. Most of all, I hope you have a renewed relationship with your Creator. Always remember, you are a miracle.

★★★

Today, sing a song of yourself. Surround yourself with things and people you love. Look in every nook and cranny of your life for joy, and like dust, blow the rest away. Forgive yourself. Embrace yourself. Just be.

Strive to experience Sabbath time every single day of your life. Whether you know it or not, you are filled with the very breath of the divine. Like Sabbath, you are a gift from our Creator.

In loving memory of my husband, Mark Hartman.

## Sunday Dinner Menu

- Reuben Casserole
- Fried Green Tomatoes
- Coffee Cake

## Rueben Casserole

### Ingredients

1/2 cup (120 g) of sour cream
1 medium onion, diced
1 (32-ounce) (960 g) can of sauerkraut, drained
2 (14.4-ounce) (435 g) cans of corn beef, crumbled
1 pound (450 g) of Swiss cheese, cubed
8 ounces (450 g) of margarine, melted

### Preparation

Grease a large casserole dish. Spread sour cream on the bottom of the dish. Layer the onion, sauerkraut, corn beef, and Swiss cheese. Drizzle with margarine.

Cook for 45 minutes at 350 degrees F (180 degrees C). Let the dish stand for 10 minutes before serving.

Serves 8. (Approximately 471 calories per serving.)

Adapted from Steve Holmer's recipe, "Reuben Casserole."

# Fried Green Tomatoes

## Ingredients

3 green tomatoes
Salt
2 cups (500 mL) of vegetable oil
1 cup (250 mL) of buttermilk
2 cups (450 g) of cornmeal

## Preparation

Slice tomatoes 1/4 inch thick. Place on a cookie sheet. Sprinkle each slice with salt. Let the tomato slice sit for 30 minutes, allowing time for the salt to draw water from the tomatoes.

Dip tomato slices in buttermilk, and then dredge in cornmeal.

In a skillet, heat the vegetable oil over medium high heat. Fry the tomato slices until golden brown.

Serves 8. (Approximately 394 calories per serving.)

# Coffee Cake

## Ingredients

1/2 cup (120 g) of shortening
1 cup (225 g) of sugar
2 eggs
1 teaspoon (5 mL) of vanilla
1/4 cup (60 mL) of 2 percent milk
1 1/2 cups (360 g) of flour
1/2 teaspoon (2.3 g) of salt
3 teaspoons (13.8 g) of baking powder
2 tablespoons (30 g) of melted margarine

## Topping For Coffee Cake

2 tablespoons (30 g) of sugar
1 teaspoon (4.6 g) of cinnamon

## Preparation

Preheat oven to 350 degrees (180 degrees C).

In a mixing bowl, cream shortening and sugar. Add eggs, vanilla, and milk. Mix well.

Add flour, salt, and baking powder to the bowl, and mix well.

Spread the batter in a 10 × 15–inch pan. Pour melted margarine over the top. Combine the sugar and cinnamon for topping. Pour melted margarine over the batter and sprinkle with sugar and cinnamon mixture.

Bake for 1 hour or until the cake surface springs back to the touch.

Serves 8. (Approximately 340 calories per serving.)

Adapted from Polly Hensley's "Coffee Cake."

Printed in the United States
By Bookmasters